BILL GULICK

Route 3, Box 319
Walla Walla, WA 99362

AUTHOR

Phone: 509 525-5882

Fiction
Bend of the River
Trails West
The Hallelujah Trail
Treasure in Hells Canyon

Northwest Destiny (a Trilogy)
Distant Trails – 1805-36
Gathering Storm – 1837-68
Lost Wallowa – 1869-79

Nonfiction
Snake River Country
Chief Joseph Country

Roadside History
of Oregon

A Traveler's History
of Washington

Manhunt:
The Pursuit of Harry Tracy

Manhunt:
The Pursuit of Harry Tracy

Bill Gulick

CAXTON PRESS
Caldwell, Idaho
1999

Copyright 1999
by Bill Gulick

Library of Congress Cataloging-in-Publication Data

Bill Gulick. 1916-
    Manhunt: The Pursuit of Harry Tracy / Bill Gulick.
        p.   cm.
    ISBN 0-87004-392-7 (pbk.)
    1. Tracy, Harry, 1870-1902. 2. Criminals—Pacific,
Northwest—Biography. 3. Prisoners—Pacific,
Northwest—Biography. 4. Fugitives from justice—Pacific,
Northwest.
    I. Title.
    HV6248.T7G85 1999
    364.15'23'097973—dc21   99-10642
                                                                CIP

Lithographed and bound in the United States of America
CAXTON PRESS
Caldwell, Idaho
164815

DEDICATION

To the intrepid reporters of 1902, who pursued Harry Tracy so relentlessly, with pencil and notebook in one hand, rifle in the other. If their aim had been as good as their writing, the chase would have ended much sooner.

vii

CONTENTS

Illustrations

Introduction

When Harry Tracy and his fellow convict David Merrill shot their way out of the Oregon State Penitentiary in Salem June 9, 1902, they initiated a manhunt unique in criminal history. A few years earlier, scholars had proclaimed the Old West dead. The telephone and telegraph wires tying the nation together had made communication instantaneous from coast to coast. The Klondike Gold Rush of 1898 had put Seattle on the map. Portland was beginning to publicize its upcoming Lewis and Clark Exposition in 1905. Urged on by William Randolph Hearst and his chain of newspapers, the United States had become a world power by fighting and winning the Spanish-American War.

Established in 1848, the Associated Press already had celebrated its fiftieth birthday. On several occasions, it had demonstrated that when a labor riot or a murder trial took place, it could put a hundred crack reporters on the scene within forty-eight hours, ready, willing, and able to lease long-lines that would transmit 10,000 words a day of lurid prose to be consumed by sensation-hungry readers in every corner of the nation.

Furthermore, photography had developed to such a point that big-city newspapers such as the Portland *Oregonian*, the Seattle *Post Intelligencer*, and the Spokane *Spokesman-Review* could have a top notch professional photographer on the scene as fast as a horse and buggy, an electric street car, or one of three transcontinental or two coastal railroad lines, which ran several fast passenger trains a day from east to west and north to south, could carry him.

Times indeed had changed. The Old West was dead. The Modern Age had come.

This being so, how could Harry Tracy avoid being captured or killed in the New West of instant communication, leading a thousand law officers, possemen, and bounty hunters on a not-so-merry chase for two months across 400 miles of western Oregon, western Washington, and across the Cascades into eastern Washington, in the process of which his partner would mysteriously disappear and he would take center stage alone by killing six of his pursuers in gun battles without suffering so much as a scratch himself?

That is the question this book will attempt to answer.

In order to do so, I have written it in the form of a dramatic narrative, taking the reader back to that place and time, letting him know only what the reader knew then, just as modern day television viewers hooked on the O.J. Simpson trial did not know what was going to happen next. Between June 9 and August 6, 1902, the millions of newspaper readers indulging their daily fix of Tracy tidbits had no inkling of what he had done until they read the paper or perused the bulletin boards posted in front of the newspaper offices, as throngs of them did.

Half a dozen times during his flight, Tracy took whole families hostage, holding them for hours or days, terrorizing them to such a degree that most of them did his bidding without question, even to the extent of not revealing his presence to the authorities until hours afterwards, as he had requested. When he moved into a house, his initial request was usually for food; his next, for the past week's newspapers, so that he could read what was being written about him.

Following his visits, the people he had held hostage became instant celebrities, giving lengthy interviews to the press, describing him as a witty, charming man, who never had harmed a woman in his life, loved children, and was very good to his horses.

Two weeks after he had killed three law officers in the Seattle area—and while he still was hiding close by—a local impresario staged a drama entitled "Tracy and Merrill," featuring a 100-member cast, starring the eighteen-year-old young lady and the teenage boy Tracy recently had held captive for a long afternoon. Assigned by the *Oregonian* to cover the Tracy story, a reporter attended and reviewed the drama, saying there was so much shooting in it ". . . deputies fell like chipmunks . . ." and that Tracy had been portrayed as such a hero that youngsters in the Seattle area surely would be inspired

"... to steal a 30-30 Winchester, shoot their parents, and then go on a rampage of kidnapping, killing, and romancing young ladies . . ."

One interesting aspect of the manhunt was that many of the reporters carried guns and became part of the posse, though none of them ever hit Tracy. Another was that no federal or state police force existed at that time to assure continuity of pursuit. To Western fans raised on *Gunsmoke* and *True Grit*, it is pointed out that while a United States marshal was authorized to pursue a fugitive within a territory, he could not do so within a state. Nor did most states have a police force of their own. Each town had a constable or town marshal; each county a sheriff and his deputies; each state a National Guard unit which the governor could mobilize in an emergency.

During the Tracy manhunt, five Oregon and Washington National Guard companies were mobilized, with the Oregon contingent actually getting into the field where the action was taking place. Sure that they had Tracy and Merrill surrounded in a patch of timber one evening and equipped with enough fire power (as one reporter wrote) to "lay down a fusillade stripping the leaves and limbs off every tree," the brave part-time soldiers did not fire a shot. When the night turned damp and cold, their part-time commander decided they would sleep better in their own beds, so at midnight, he sent them home, despite the protests of the local sheriff, who had no authority over them. When daylight came, Tracy and Merrill were gone.

When a fugitive moved from one county to another, the jurisdiction of one sheriff ended and that of another began, requiring a complete change in authority. Only in King County, which included the populous city of Seattle, was the budget large enough to let Sheriff Edward Cudihee—three of whose deputies had been killed by Tracy—spend $10,000 of taxpayer money during the manhunt, and to swear—as he did—that he would follow Tracy "to the ends of the earth," no matter how far the trail led outside the sheriff's King County jurisdiction.

For his failure to capture or kill Tracy while the outlaw was making headlines in the Seattle area, Sheriff Cudihee was ridiculed by the press. Why he did not strike back by caustically asking the reporters why none of them had managed to hit

Tracy the numerous times they shot at him may only be attributed to his savvy as a politician, who knew better than to get sarcastic with reporters. On several occasions, it should be noted, when reporters inadvertently mistook one another for Tracy and exchanged shots, their aim continued to be bad.

But he did stay with the chase to its bitter end, asked for no part of the reward money, but did manage to persuade Washington's Governor McBride to let him route the coffin of the dead outlaw through Seattle on its way back to Salem, Oregon, just to show his constituents that he had lived up to his reputation of always getting his man.

Though there are comic elements in the prolonged manhunt, there was nothing humorous then or now in the fact that Harry Tracy killed seven men during his flight toward freedom, most of whom left grieving widows and fatherless children, in an age when there was no workman's compensation, pensions, or survivors' benefits. One of the dead Oregon prison guards, for example, left a widow and eight children, while an inmate whose leg was shattered by a bullet when he tried to prevent the escape, spent seven weeks in the hospital after his leg was amputated, then was turned loose with a pardon but no compensation, being forced to face the bleak prospect of making his living in a world that had no use for a one-legged ex-con.

For the most part, I have resisted the temptation to point out similarities between then and now, so far as the public's fascination with chase scenes, criminals, violence, and media coverage are concerned. If the reader is inclined to smile at the spectacle of a dozen reporters hopping into a carryall and tooling across the dusty plain with a deputy and his posse at word of a Tracy sighting, I will agree that it must have looked ridiculous. Of course, when the Marines landed on a Somalia beach a few years ago and found that the bright lights shining in their eyes were being held for the benefit of TV cameras and anchormen—well, that was media coverage as practiced today. At least, the reporters were not armed.

As for the souvenir hunters who stripped Tracy's blood-soaked body and hacked splinters from his coffin, such behavior 100 years ago must be condemned as unenlightened. In these more intelligent times—such as at the Simpson trial, were

licenses required and designated curbside vendor spots set
aside for specialty item sales people.

At the end of this book, I intend to list the newspaper sources
I have used and mention some of the articles and books I have
read about Harry Tracy's life and times. But the text that
immediately follows is nothing more or less than the "Chase
Scene," which began when he went over the wall and ending
with his burial—which is probably all we will ever know or
want to know about his violent, bloody career.

—Bill Gulick

ACKNOWLEDGEMENTS

As noted earlier, the primary sources for this book have been 1902 newspaper accounts by reporters who were there "when the guns went off," so to speak. This has meant many hours of using microfilm readers and printers at research facilities such as Penrose Library, Whitman College in Walla Walla, the Public Library in Spokane, the *Wenatchee World* and North Central Washington Historical Society Museum in Wenatchee, and the Chelan County Historical Society Museum in Chelan.

For the use of their excellent equipment and the helpful expertise of their staffs, I am most grateful.

Particular thanks are due Henry Yapel, Librarian, Larry Dodd, Archivist, and Marilyn Sparks, Research Specialist, at Penrose Library for their guidance in finding material I might otherwise have missed. An equal debt is owed to Mark Behler, Curator, North Central Historical Society, Wilfred Woods, publisher emeritus, and Linda Barta, Librarian, *Wenatchee World*, and to Marcelle Carpenter, Historical Museum in Chelan.

The important role played by museums and historical societies certainly deserves mention here, for without them much regional material would be lost. Staffed by unpaid volunteers whose hobby is history, given a bit of guidance by a professional curator or archivist, working with minimum funding and often housed in buildings that are themselves historical monuments, these museums contain real treasures. Having visited many of them and worked with their people during the thirty-five years I have been researching and writing regional history, I appreciate their value.

In addition to those already mentioned, others in eastern Washington worth visiting are the Douglas County Museum in Waterville and the Fort Walla Walla Museum in Walla Walla, where my long-time friend, Bill Lake, has sold a lot of my books in the Museum store. James Payne, the present director, and Jackie Russell, photo archivist, are just beginning to catalog the treasures in their files, one of which is a diagram of the Oregon boot.

So far as Harry Tracy landmarks or museums are concerned, the principal one is in Davenport, where the Lincoln County Museum has a case displaying his frying pan, some of the cartridges from his rifle, a death mask, several photos of his corpse before and after being embalmed, and the Eddy ranch site where he was killed. At Creston, a few miles west, the City Hall has several Tracy photos and can give directions to Tracy Rock on the former Eddy ranch, though going there requires permission from the current owner of the property.

Because the newspapers in which I did my research were so profusely illustrated with excellent photographs of everyone involved in the manhunt, I did not anticipate that getting copies of those photos would be much of a problem. But it turned out to be a serious one. In 1902, a skilled photographer using either glass plate or silver-impregnated paper film could take excellent pictures if the light were right and the subject could be persuaded to hold still long enough so the photos reproduced in the newspapers of the day were very clear. But the notion that these photos might have historical value and should be carefully preserved seems to have occurred to few editors, historical societies, or even to the photographers themselves.

Time and again I was told horror stories such as how a collection of a hundred or so 8" X 10" glass plates had been used as panels in a greenhouse after the death of the photographer who had taken them by a descendant who was more interested in raising flowers than preserving priceless pictures. All too often when a big-city newspaper moved into larger quarters, it gave only a small percentage of its photographs to the local historical society, then trashed the rest.

Going through the one-hundred-year-old files of the newspapers themselves, then hiring a professional photographer to copy each and every photo I wanted to use, was not possible because of budget limitations. So I did the next best thing, which was to get the best prints possible from the microfilmed newspapers, then hope that they could be computer-enhanced to the point of reasonable clarity.

In any case, for their valiant efforts to find photographs I could use, I thank Susie Reynolds, Seattle Public Library, Carolyn Marr, Museum of History and Industry in Seattle, Photo Archivist John Mead at the Oregon Historical Society, and Dave Wendell, Oregon State Archives, Salem, Oregon, and the staff of the Washington State Library in Olympia.

Finally, I acknowledge the assistance and support of my wife, Jeanne, who, as a retired Penrose librarian, corrected me every time I made a historical mistake, and was always ready to hit the road on a research trip the moment I jingled the car keys.

—Bill Gulick

CHAPTER ONE
OVER THE WALL

A t the state penitentiary in Salem, Oregon, in 1902, the authorities believed in making the inmates do useful work, insisting that they start their day early. That was why guards S.R.T. Jones and B.F. Tiffany, who were in charge of the foundry workshop where iron stoves were being manufactured, finished roll call by 7 a.m. the morning of June 9, reported all prisoners present or accounted for, then marched their contingent of 165 men from the chapel into the foundry building, where Guard F.B. Ferrell would supervise their work.

But two of the most dangerous inmates, Harry Tracy and David Merrill, had made other plans for the day—escape and flight to freedom—even if they had to kill any man who stood in their way.

As the inmates were being marched along an aisle where sheet metal, tools, and materials were stacked, the two men suddenly stooped, picked up Winchester rifles and Colt revolvers which had been stashed there by friendly visitors or recently released convicts, and came up shooting. Since prison regulations required that foundry guards be unarmed, the only thing the guards could do was flee along the aisle.

Dropping to one knee, Harry Tracy—a crack shot who had killed at least three men before being sentenced to a twenty-year prison term for armed robbery three years earlier—fired a single rifle bullet, that struck Ferrell in the back, killing him instantly.

Hearing the shot, Frank Gerard, another guard, looked quickly around, saw the two armed men coming toward him, and took flight, running for his life down the aisle, while his two pursuers gained on him at every step. Then, for some inexplicable reason, Frank Inghram, a life prisoner from Linn County, seeing the peril in which the guard was placed, stepped out and attempted to stop the escaping men.

David Merrill, who was also a good shot, paused long enough to fire at Inghram, the bullet striking the inmate in the knee and damaging it so badly that the leg later had to be amputated. Firing shot after shot at Gerard and John Stapleton, another guard who was in the foundry, the convicts continued on their way. Their intended victims sought shelter in the prison yard and were safe for the time being.

Getting out of the foundry building, Tracy and Merrill again brought their murderous rifles into play. First, they riddled the extreme southwest and northwest guard posts, but fortunately did not kill anyone. Then, with a single shot at a distance of 150 yards, Tracy brought down Jones, who was on the wall in charge of the north post. As the guard fell dead, the two convicts turned and took several shots at Tiffany and Ross, guards on the north wall, but other than piercing Ross's hat, inflicted no damage.

Believing that they had sufficiently impressed the guards with the accuracy of their fire, the two convicts secured a ladder from one of the buildings, placed it against the east wall, then mounted it, while bullets fired by guards on the walls flew thick and fast all around them. Tiffany, who had not lost his nerve, repeatedly sent shots after them, none of which reached their mark. An instant later, the two men jumped down from the wall and disappeared.

Running along to the spot where the men had crossed, Tiffany and Ross leaped after them and followed them around an angle in the wall, where they met face-to-face. Instantly, the guards were covered and commanded to give up their rifles and cartridges. With the memory of the murders that had already been done fresh in their minds, the guards complied and threw their guns and ammunition on the ground.

Taken as hostages and ordered to march just ahead of the

escaping men, the two guards shuffled along with their hands in the air for a hundred yards. Then a guard stationed at a post on a distant wall unwisely fired a shot at the fugitives.

Instantly, the two convicts returned the fire, and Tiffany, who one of them had selected as a target, fell dead, with a bullet through his right breast. Ross immediately dropped, and his presence of mind saved his life, for the men, believing that he, too, had been killed, paid no further attention to the shots behind them and ran for cover.

Inside the foundry and the other buildings of the penitentiary, the spectacle of the dead guards and the wounded convict forced a pall of silence on the general population of the prison. Huddled together in paralyzed groups, the inmates showed by their immobility that this was not a concerted escape attempt. However the break for freedom had been arranged, Harry Tracy and David Merrill were entirely on their own.

One of the mysteries of the escape was who had supplied the weapons used by the convicts and how they had been placed where they could be found? The Portland *Oregonian* printed one theory:

> *Warden J.T. Janes says he is satisfied the rifles and ammunition with which Tracy and Merrill were provided were smuggled into the prison inclosure and into the shops either Saturday night or Sunday night. Warden Janes says he is positive the work was done by an ex-convict, Harry Wright, in accordance with a prearranged plan that was formulated before Wright was released. He thinks a place and time were designated for hiding the weapons within the shop, and that the plans were perfectly carried into execution. The force of guards at the Penitentiary, particularly the night force, is not large enough to prevent outside interference. There is but one outside night guard at the Penitentiary, and it would not be a difficult matter for a confederate to scale the prison walls during the night, deposit firearms within the inclosure, and escape undetected.*

Another report circulated that the weapons were passed into the prison the previous Sunday by members of a party of excursionists who visited the institution, but this was vigorously denied by the penitentiary officials, who claimed that not the slightest opportunity was presented on Sunday for the delivery of firearms or anything else to the prisoners.

"It is the supposition," the warden said, "that since Tracy and Merrill are prominently identified with an organized gang of criminals, they received outside assistance this morning that will make more difficult their capture."

Called by the police the two most desperate criminals on the Pacific Coast, Harry Tracy and David Merrill had both been sent to the Salem penitentiary from Multnomah County for numerous cases of highway robbery. In 1899, Tracy had been sentenced to twenty years, Merrill to thirteen, after terrorizing the Portland area for several years. The crimes for which they had been convicted were as petty as they were brutal.

One of their first robberies was an attack on a Second Street trolley car. They took the conductor's watch, and relieved sundry passengers of their valuables. Later, they stormed Dr. Plummer's drug store at Third and Madison streets, held up the clerk, bound and gagged him, and stole postage stamps. They went into Russell's Saloon on East Clay and Grand, tied Russell's hands behind his back and jammed a towel in his mouth and halfway down his throat, hammering it in with the butt ends of their revolvers.

Magoon's Saloon, Sixth and Ankeny, also was robbed by the pair, who stole an overcoat, a watch and chain, and money. Other robberies by Tracy and Merrill included: Jennings, Sixth and Clay; Otto Neussler's Saloon, Eleventh and Washington; Wey's Butcher Shop, Fourth Street; Barrett's Butcher Shop, Front and Gibbs Streets; and Offner, a grocer at Fourth and Lincoln.

The method invariably used by Merrill and Tracy was to enter stores with revolvers in their hands, in daylight, and demand money and valuables, which, if not given up, brought on a beating.

Merrill's description at the time of his arrest February 5,

1899, was: "Stands 5'-11", age 28, 100 pounds, blue eyes, fair hair, light mustache, four front teeth missing in upper jaw, and two vaccination marks on left arm. Arrested on Market Street, near Front."

Tracy's description was: "Stands 5'-10", twenty-five years old. 160 pounds, gray eyes, light hair and mustache, vaccination marks on left arm and scar left by bullet on left leg. Arrested at Fifth and Hall Street."

The detectives who ran down and arrested Tracy and Merrill later told an interesting story about their capture:

Early in February, 1899, the police received information that the two men were in Mrs. Merrill's house, on Market Street near First. Their capture was assigned to Detectives Cordano and Ford.

Accompanied by Policeman Banks, Cordano went to take a look at the house late at night. Since both Merrill and Tracy were known to be deadly shots, it was decided to postpone the arrests until daylight. Next day, Detective Ford guarded the front door, while Policemen Warner, Jameson, and Banks each watched a window. In the event that Merrill and Tracy attempted to escape, the law officers were authorized to shoot to kill.

Cordano assumed the position of the most danger, the back door, for it was known that when Mrs. Merrill heard a knock on the front door, she would call out, "Come in!", a signal for her son and his outlaw friends to run out the back door.

The formula worked as expected. When Ford knocked on the front door, Cordano heard the sound of running footsteps inside the house. A moment later, David Merrill flung open the back door, found himself gazing into the muzzle of Cordano's revolver, slammed the door shut, and locked it.

Breaking down the door, Detective Cordano burst into the house, where he met Detective Ford, who had knocked in the front door.

"Where's your man?" Ford demanded.

"I don't see him," Cordano replied. "But he's got to be somewhere inside the house."

As the two officers began their search, neither Mrs. Merrill nor her younger son, Ben, who was sitting with her in the living room, made any objection until they approached a door leading to what appeared to be a small spare bedroom.

"What's in here?" Cordano asked.

"Nothing much," Mrs. Merrill answered evasively. "You don't need to go in there."

"Yes, I do. Open the door for me, young man."

"Not me," Ben said nervously. "Ain't nothin' worth seein' in there."

"If you don't open this door, I'll break it down."

Apprehensively, the young man opened the door, then stepped quickly to one side, as if expecting fireworks. Entering the room, Detective Cordano found that it contained nothing but a bedstead, a carpet, and a bureau of drawers standing against the far wall. Suspecting that the room was not as empty as it appeared to be, Detective Cordano pulled out the lower bureau drawer far enough to expose the tip of a shoe inside. Pulling out the drawer just above it to use as a shield, Cordano drew his revolver, then jerked open the lower drawer so that he could inspect its contents. Lying curled up on his back with a .44 caliber revolver in his hand was the skinny figure of David Merrill—who weighed only 100 pounds, but still had to be something of a contortionist to have crammed his five-foot, eleven-inch body inside the drawer.

"Throw up your hands!" Cordano ordered.

Confined as he was, David Merrill could not reach very high, but sight of the detective's revolver in his face discouraged any impulse he might have had to resist.

"Give up or you die right here!" Cordano exclaimed.

Merrill surrendered. As he was being disarmed and hand-cuffed, Mrs. Merrill ran into the room, sobbing hysterically.

"Don't take my son away! He is not a criminal!"

When Detective Cordano showed by his actions that he thought otherwise, Mrs. Merrill's appeal for mercy took a different tack. "If I tell you something that will help you arrest Harry Tracy, will you give me half of the reward?"

"My job is to arrest criminals, ma'am," Detective Cordano said politely, "not to share rewards. But I will appreciate any information you can give me."

After admitting that David Merrill had threatened to kill

her and his younger brother, Ben, if either of them ever gave
him away to the law, Mrs. Merrill proved the old adage "there
is no honor among thieves" by telling Detective Cordano that
Harry Tracy planned to visit the house on February 6, just a
day or two hence. If the authorities would keep the arrest of
David Merrill a secret, which they promised they would do, she
said she would let the law officers set up an ambush inside the
house and capture the unsuspecting wanted man when he
appeared. If a reward were to be given for Tracy's arrest, she
hoped for a fair share of it.

The ambush was arranged, with Detectives Cordano, Ford,
and Weiner taking turns at waiting inside the Merrill house,
pretending to be friends visiting the Merrill family. In
mid-afternoon February 6, Detective Weiner relieved Cordano
and Ford so that they could go out and get something to eat.
Hardly had the two officers left the house when a man wearing
a black mackintosh, which was Harry Tracy's usual garb,
walked into the room with a familiarity that showed he was a
habitual guest here.

So smooth was Weiner's manner that Tracy believed him to
be a friend of the Merrill family. Not wanting to make an arrest
that might cause gunplay inside the house, Weiner suggested a
walk to the corner, to which Tracy agreed. Though the conversation between the two men still was casual, Tracy grew
increasingly suspicious after they had walked a few blocks.
When they approached the corner of Fourth and Market, Tracy
noticed a Southern Pacific passenger train moving slowly along
the tracks just ahead, gestured at it, and said,

"See that train. Guess I'll take it. So long."

"I guess you won't," Detective Weiner disagreed, throwing
open his coat to reveal his badge and drawing his revolver to
reinforce his statement. "You're under arrest, Mr. Tracy,
charged with felonious assault, armed robbery, unprovoked
brutality producing bodily harm, and numerous other crimes . .
."

The lightning reflexes which triggered Harry Tracy's movements then and on many future occasions when officers
attempting to arrest him talked rather than acted, impelled the
wanted man away from Detective Weiner before the officer

could cock his pistol. Drawing his own gun, Tracy sent two bullets whistling past the officer's head. Both shots missed, as did the two fired by Weiner at the fugitive.

Reaching the engine of the slowly moving train, Tracy jumped aboard, placed the muzzle of his revolver against the engineer's head, and ordered, "High-ball it, buddy—or you're a dead man!"

Having witnessed the attempt of Detective Weiner, who happened to be a good friend, to arrest Harry Tracy, and the exchange of gunfire that had followed, the engineer responded not by opening up the throttle as Tracy had demanded but by pulling the cord on the emergency air-brake system, which, with a hiss of steam, locked all the wheels the length of the train and brought it to a squealing stop.

"Sorry, friend," the iron-nerved engineer told Tracy. "Control of the train has passed out of my hands."

Realizing that shooting the engineer would do him no good, Tracy leaped down from the cab and began running along Harrison Street. By now, the entire neighborhood had been alerted to the fact that the notorious Harry Tracy had tried to kill the detective who was attempting to arrest him, so was fair game for any man who might be lucky enough to shoot him down, whether a professional or an amateur. Since in that place and time, most business establishments and houses were well stocked with firearms and occupied by men who knew how to use them, the streets soon were filled with hunters looking for a target.

Credit for the first wing shot to take effect on Tracy, later participants in the shootout agreed, probably should be given to a man named Albert Way, whose double-barreled shotgun was loaded with number four lead pellets—a charge that would sting but not kill at the hundred-yard range at which he plunked Tracy in the back of the head. Momentarily confused, the fleeing man blundered into a yard guarded by Policeman Wilkinson, who nearly got him with a revolver shot, then whirled around and ran directly into the arms and pistol range of Detective Weiner, who this time had the good sense to shorten his arrest statement to:

"Surrender or die!"

And this time, Tracy surrendered.

Such were the circumstances surrounding the arrest, trial, and sentencing of Harry Tracy and David Merrill on March 21, 1899. During the three years they spent as fellow prisoners at the Oregon State Penitentiary, Tracy seems to have had no inkling of the role David Merrill's mother had played in his betrayal and capture, though in the weeks to come he would learn of it by reading Detective Cordano's account in the *Oregonian*—with serious consequences to David Merrill.

Meantime, pursuit of the two escaped prisoners was beginning in earnest. News of the break spread rapidly. By the hundreds, the citizens of Salem, which was the state capital, armed themselves with rifles, pistols, or shotguns, then offered their services as posse members to Sheriff Durbin and Chief of Police Gibson. Splotches of blood on the ground in the direction the convicts had taken indicated that at least one of them had been wounded. If so, the injury was not severe, for the two fleeing men made their way rapidly up Mill Creek, along which the brush was very thick, then turned into it and disappeared.

When last seen around noon by a farmer named John Baumann, two miles southeast of Salem, they were still wearing their prison clothes, were packing the rifles they had picked up in the shop and taken from the guards, and were carrying a sack presumed to contain revolvers and ammunition. As the day passed, none of the searching parties was able to locate them, though reports that they had been spotted in one place or another constantly trickled in.

"We're not worried about keeping track of them," said one law officer, who refused to be quoted by name, "because we know they'll leave a trail when they hold up a farmer for food or clothes, which they're going to need. Bloodhounds are on the way from the state prison at Walla Walla, due to get here at eleven o'clock tomorrow morning. Take my word for it, we'll either have those two murderers brought back to answer for their crimes or stretched out cold on the ground before dark tomorrow."

Because three guards had been killed during the escape, Penitentiary Superintendent J.D. Lee announced that a reward of $500 would be paid for the capture of Harry Tracy, who was believed to have done most of the shooting. When public indignation demanded that the amount be increased to $1,000, with no restrictions as to whether "capture" meant alive or dead, a few state bureaucrats briefly wondered if such an expenditure of funds would be approved. But such doubts were quickly put to rest when a group of prominent local citizens, headed by R.J. Hendricks, declared:

> *If the State of Oregon won't pay it, we'll personally guarantee the thousand dollars ourselves. And we won't object one bit if the State is spared the expense of a trial.*

In addition to the posses fanning out over the area to search for the two escapees, Company "F" of the Oregon National Guard, was mustered into service, with its forty members under the command of Captain H.A. Kurtz gaining valuable field experience by spreading out around Salem to help form a ring of steel through which no fugitives could possibly slip.

"The boys had their first experience of cross-country marching," a reporter wrote sympathetically, "and arrived home quite fatigued."

Meantime, newspaper stories detailing the criminal background of Harry Tracy and David Merrill were being published, beginning the legend-building process. Policemen who knew them said both men were unusually good shots. Tracy often performed the trick, one policeman said, of throwing a tin can twenty feet into the air, then riddling it with bullets before it struck the ground. Though David Merrill's mother, who had betrayed Tracy after her son had been arrested several years ago, had since died, Tracy had been married to David Merrill's sister at the time of his arrest. That worthy lady had remained loyal to her husband despite her mother's treachery, managing to smuggle a pistol into Tracy's cell while he was being held in a Portland jail, which he had attempted to use in an aborted escape. That the attempt failed must be credited to the courage of an unusually brave jailer, who told Tracy when the outlaw pointed the pistol at his head and demanded that the cell be unlocked:

"Go ahead and shoot me. It won't do you a bit of good. When

the other guards come running and see what you've done, you'll die right in your cell."

Believing the jailer meant what he said, Tracy gave up the gun.

One of the intriguing stories told about Tracy and Merrill was that both men were members of the "Hole-in-the-Wall" gang down in Utah, later to be made famous by Butch Cassidy and the Sundance Kid. It was said they had taken part in the murder of a sheriff in Salt Lake City. Though most historians place the "Hole-in-the-Wall" hideout in Wyoming, there apparently were "wild bunches" in both places, with outlaw trails extending into New Mexico.

In 1897, Tracy was sentenced to a term of one year in the Utah State Penitentiary for burglary, but remained in captivity only two months before managing to escape. Taken out with a work gang to a rock quarry one morning, Tracy and three other convicts were under the charge of Guard John Van Stetter, who was armed with a double-barreled shotgun. Persuading Van Stetter that he had bent his shovel and needed help to fix it, Tracy got the gullible guard to come far enough into the circle of the four men that his long-barreled shotgun could not be brought into play. Tracy then drew a revolver concealed in his convict's jacket and placed its muzzle against the guard's head.

"Drop the shotgun! That's a good fellow! Now take off your clothes."

After John Van Stetter had stripped to the buff, Harry Tracy took off his convict garb, put on the uniform, picked up the double-barreled shotgun, and escorted his three fellow prisoners away from the rock quarry work site as if he had the authority to do so, keeping the guard covered with the revolver until the convicts passed from his view. Naked, unarmed, and barefoot, the de-fanged guard made no effort to pursue. Though posses later scoured the country, no trace of the prisoners ever was found.

After leaving the quarry, the escapees split up, with Tracy and a man named Lant going east in the direction of Parley's Canyon. There, they held up a man and his wife driving a buggy, used it to get to western Colorado, where, after a few weeks, Harry Tracy killed a young rancher for whom he had worked for a while, then quarreled with. By then, Tracy and Lant had parted company, but with his usual indifference to evading the scene or consequences of his crimes, Tracy was captured by local law officers and placed in jail to await trial. Disliking the quality of his confinement, he beat three guards into insensibility and escaped. Re-taken in a day or so, he was kept in custody, this time for two weeks, when he again escaped after almost killing a guard by clubbing him over the head with an improvised blackjack.

Since the Colorado escape, nothing had been heard from Tracy until he surfaced in Portland, went on a burglary spree with David Merrill, and was sentenced to prison for misdeeds committed with his partner.

At the time of his escape in 1902, Tracy's age was recorded as twenty-five, so his first brush with the law must have occurred in 1897, when he was barely twenty years old.

As more information about the escape was circulated, it became apparent that the motive of revenge had played a leading part in the killings of guards Tiffany and Ferrell. During the time of their incarceration, prison officials said, the two men had been indolent, disagreeable, and considered so dangerous that they often were required to wear "Oregon Boots," heavily weighted high-topped shoes which greatly restricted movement.

"Their deportment was so bad," one official said, "that the guards who were overseers in the foundry frequently had to report them, with the result that the management often punished the refractory prisoners. Thus, in discharging their duty, Ferrell and Tiffany incurred the enmity of these two convicts, who took their revenge."

Oregon State Archives, Salem, Ore.

Harry Tracy in 1899, when he was sentenced to
twenty years in prison.

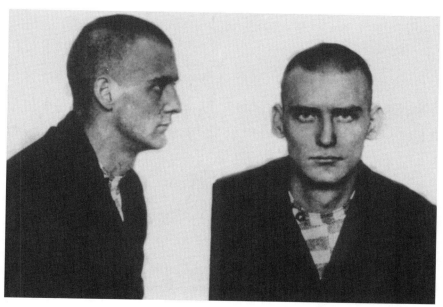

Oregon State Archives, Salem, Ore.

David Merril, in 1899, when he received
a fifteen-year prison sentence.

Oregon Historical Society

Looking north on Fifth Street in Portland, about 1900. A year earlier, Harry Tracy and David Merrill were sent to prison after a two-man crime spree in Oregon's largest city.

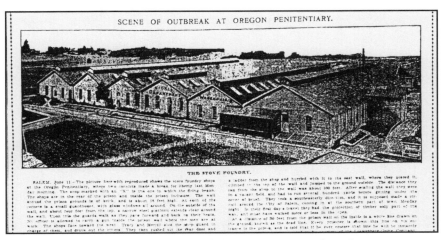

Newspaper drawing of the prison stove foundry, where the convicts began their escape attempt.

Chapter Two

THE PURSUIT BEGINS

The assumption by the authorities that Tracy and Merrill would hold up a farmer in remote back country for food and clothes proved to be as erroneous as their belief that the "ring of steel" created by the numerous posses and Company "F" of the National Guard would be leak-proof. By no means a novice at the escape business, Tracy long ago had learned the wisdom of doing exactly the opposite of what he was expected to do.

Instead of continuing to flee up Mill Creek, he and Merrill doubled back toward the center of Salem as soon as darkness fell, evading their pursuers by appearing to be part of a posse. When they did steal clothes, their victim was not a farmer but a town resident in whom they inspired so much fear that he waited from 10 p.m., when the robbery occurred, until four a.m. to report it because he believed their threat to do him bodily harm if he talked any sooner.

"I had just returned home about ten o'clock last evening from downtown," J.W. Roberts told a reporter, "and as I entered the gate at my home I observed two men approaching me. I presumed they were members of the searching parties returning home, and I paused to question them. In an instant I found myself covered with two rifles, and I obeyed the command of 'Hands up and be quiet!' The men were both dressed in the garb of convicts, and asked if I was an officer of the law.

"They then stated that their names were Tracy and Merrill, the escaped prisoners from the penitentiary. They made me remove my hat, coat, vest and trousers, which they divided between themselves, having discarded one convict's shirt and a pair of black trousers. After warning me not to alarm the police, the men left. They had the latest modern improved rifles with plenty of ammunition, and said they were prepared to fight to a finish, for they would never surrender alive."

Shortly thereafter, the two fugitives stole a team from a resident named Felix LaBranch, who said he had put a pair of Clydesdale draft horses, each weighing 1,200 pounds, in the barn at 9 p.m., then found the barnyard gate and door open and the animals missing when he went to get them at four o'clock in the morning. Some people speculated that the horses had been stolen by confederates and given to Tracy and Merrill; but that theory was abandoned when officers pointed out that fugitives as daring as these had proved themselves to be did not need any assistance.

During the next few days, as a matter of fact, Tracy and Merrill were seen, reported, or shown by thefts attributed to them to be in so many locations that no confederates could possibly have kept up with, let alone aided, them. At 9:30 the next evening, they showed up at the home of Alonzo Briggs, who lived in the small town of Gervais a few miles north of the "ring of steel" with which the authorities thought they had encircled Salem. After forcing Briggs at gunpoint to cook and serve them a meal, they next appeared in an alley in back of the drug store and post office on Main Street.

Climbing a fence, they passed through the back yard of the residence of E. Bupease, then between two hotels. On the street nearby, they met and held up a buggy containing two members of a posse which was looking for them, forcing the men in it to give up their guns and coats. The chagrined posse members were then forced out of the buggy, which the two fugitives took and drove toward the outskirts of town. Ten minutes later, the horse returned with the empty buggy.

Several citizens saw the convicts in town, it was later learned, but none attempted to capture them. Sheriff Durbin soon came up, and with two bloodhounds from the Walla Walla penitentiary, in charge of Guard E.M.Carson, again set out in pursuit.

If the much bally-hooed Washington bloodhounds and their highly-praised handler failed to live up to their advance billing, the same criticism must be made of the supposedly skilled newspaper reporters who were covering the chase and trying to clarify what was happening for the enlightenment of their readers. When it came to tracking flight and pursuit, both bloodhounds and reporters frequently lost the trail. A journalist wrote:

> *Dr. P.S. White and Ed Bupease, a farmer, were the men in the buggy. They were returning to Gervais with Sheriff Durbin's posse. Both men were armed. White's conveyance was but a few yards from that of the Sheriff. The posse at Gervais, which was organized at Salem, started after the men at 6 o'clock, picking up the scent where the men had been seen in the morning by August King, a woodchopper.*
>
> *King was surprised by the fugitives at 4 o'clock this morning while cooking breakfast. He was ordered to serve them, which he did, not aware that they were wanted for murder. At noon Mr. Miller, King's employer, arrived, and on learning of the visitors, notified the authorities. The posse did not arrive until almost dusk. The bloodhounds were baffled for a time, but finally scented Merrill's trail, and ran it for almost a mile, where it was lost.*

Here, Sheriff Durbin and the reporter also became lost, so far as locating the fleeing men was concerned. Believing he had the escapees surrounded, Sheriff Durbin set up a "skirmish line" around a patch of timber, sure that he had his quarry trapped inside. Thinking Tracy to be wounded, stiff and sore from his day's exertions, the sheriff felt attempting to flush the two desperate men out of the timber in the darkness would be the height of folly. Posting a few guards on the roads outside the patch of timber, Sheriff Durbin gave the rest of the posse members permission to go to their homes in Gervais for the night.

"Come daybreak, we'll flush them out," he said confidentally. "Ain't no doubt about that."

But the fugitives were not in the patch of timber. Instead, they were in Gervais, which was where they held up Dr. White and Ed Bupease, taking their rifles, coats, and buggy.

"The rest of the posse was within gunshot," a reporter wrote, "but did not know what had happened until the fugitives had a fair start."

Again putting the bloodhounds on the trail, which they soon lost, Sheriff Durbin reached the not particularly brilliant conclusion that the object of the men riding a short distance in Dr. White's buggy no doubt had been to throw the bloodhounds off their track.

"The dogs trace them easily enough when on damp ground," the sheriff said. "But in the dry dust they soon lose the scent."

This trouble having been experienced in and about Salem to a marked degree, the dogs were taken to the penitentiary and allowed to sniff the bedding of the escaped convicts in the hope of giving them a better scent. By then, of course, the escapees had changed clothes.

Apparently liking the cooking at the woodchopper's camp, Tracy and Merrill astonished August King by again showing up at four o'clock the next morning and demanding that he fix them another breakfast.

"They came to my place an hour ago," King told Sheriff Durbin after hastening to town to inform the authorities of the unexpected repeat visit, "and wanted something to eat. They were very polite, and offered to pay any price I wanted for some food. All I had was a loaf of bread, which they received."

This time, they did not sit down, as they had done the day before, holding their guns all the while, even poking the barrel of a rifle into a bunk inside the shack to make sure no one was concealed there. When King first opened the door to their knock, Tracy said, "Partner, I suppose you know who we are."

King said that he did, and advised them not to stay long, as the posse was after them. "They cautioned me not to raise an alarm or notify the officers, and then departed."

At 5:30 a.m., with the early summer dawn just breaking, Sheriff Durbin and his men started for King's place with the bloodhounds, intent upon having the dogs take up this fresh scent. Determined to organize today's search in a more systematic manner, Durbin posted pickets along the roads, as on the preceding night, this time sure that the fugitives were within the loop. Soon, the dogs were on the scent again, following it intermittently through the belt of timber on what was called the Miller place. Though the hounds tracked the two men easily enough along the inside of the fence on the graveyard road, where the earth was moist, they lost it on a dry patch of ground, milling around uncertainly.

"There was a standstill in the search for the time being, pending the arrival of reinforcements," wrote the *Oregonian* reporter, without explaining why reinforcements were needed when the problem was a lost trail. "These came on the first train from Salem, when 18 young men, the majority members of the Oregon National Guard, came, armed. On the second morning train from the capitol were 12 men, all known to be expert shots. These reinforcements were transported to the scene of action at once, and were assigned to guard duty along the roads by Sheriff Durbin."

With the two bloodhounds now properly backed up, their handler, Guard Carson, turned them loose in the thick woods to re-discover the trail. Though it took the dogs several exhausting hours to do so, they at last picked it up, following it through dense brush and over a recent burn into a marsh deep in the timber.

"Here the scent was again lost," the reporter wrote, "and the game stood at a standstill until the afternoon."

By now, the hard-working bloodhounds were footsore, worn out, and badly in need of a rest, with no replacements available. But the supply of human trackers was inexhaustible.

Oregon Governor T.T. Greer notified Sheriff Durbin that he would call out the militia, if it was deemed necessary to increase the number of pursuers. When his offer was promptly accepted by the sheriff, Company "M," at Woodburn, and Company "D," at Salem, were sent to the front as quickly as possible. During the afternoon, the militiamen arrived and were assigned to posts along the roads, thereby doubling the number of guards. Every point of vantage now was occupied by an armed man, Sheriff Durbin told reporters, whose up-to-the-hour news flashes brought noncombatants flocking to the area to gawk, get in the way, and await developments.

"It's evident that the men are in the timber," Sheriff Durbin said. "Starving them out is the most plausible plan."

At 2:45 p.m. a ripple of excitement ran over the watchers when Eugene Fisher, a Salem militiaman, reported seeing Tracy and Merrill in a wheat field adjacent to the stand of timber in which they were thought to be hiding.

"The news spread like wildfire," a reporter wrote, "and the Woodburn militia was taken to the field in a conveyance."

Presumably rested now and also taken by conveyance to the scene, the bloodhounds went back to work. A search "of strenuous interest" resumed. Immediately, the dogs picked up a hot trail, keeping their noses close to the ground and baying eagerly as they dragged Guard Carson, who was holding their leashes, in the direction they wanted to go.

The trail led the pursuers into a shady lane, which suddenly dipped into a gully. Before descending, Carson glanced at the other side through the tree branches, and saw a natural barricade of stones across the path. Fearing an ambuscade, he talked with Sheriff Durbin, who entertained similar views.

A halt was called. Dave Sullivan, one of the posse members, was pursuing the chase so enthusiastically that he had become reckless; now he was infecting other men in the group with a heedless desire to press on. Sheriff Durbin was more cautious, commanding that all posse members return, stating that it was useless to proceed and sacrifice good lives for those of the men in hiding.

After protesting strongly, the posse agreed to hold back. The pursuers had only begun to retreat when shots were fired at them from behind the barricade. The plan of the fugitives was now apparent. They wished to tempt their pursuers to attack, the latter having the disadvantage of charging over open ground while the convicts lay unseen behind the pile of rocks.

Prudently, Sheriff Durbin declined to attack the stronghold, letting his forces, which now numbered 250 men, bang away as they saw fit, with Tracy and Merrill now and then returning a shot to show they had not been hit. Noting that the men surrounding the two convicts were equipped with 45-70 caliber Springfield rifles, a reporter calculated that if a broadside were fired it "would mow down the forest like a cyclone, and leave not a tree standing beneath which the fugitives could hide their shaven heads."

Instead of letting loose such a barrage, the militiamen and posse members sent just enough bullets buzzing into the cover to disturb the sleep of the outlaws. Around two o'clock in the morning, Tracy and Merrill decided to get up and move out, managing, as they always seemed able to do, to slip unseen and unheard through the cordon of guards encircling them.

Proof that they had done so came in the form of a 7 a.m. phone call from the town of Monitor, five miles way, with the news that they had breakfasted there. When told that his birds had flown their nest, Sheriff Durbin alerted the militia, the posse members, Guard Carson and the bloodhounds, all of whom began the process of moving to the new scene of action. Soon the bloodhounds were scouring the banks of Pudding Creek for fresh scent of their quarry, while posse members and militiamen followed.

"It was not later than noon," the reporter wrote, "when the Salem company proceeded to Monitor, where they stayed until the dews began to fall, in a state of innocuous, but enjoyable desuetude."

That the escapees had indeed taken breakfast in Monitor was confirmed rather testily by Mrs. Barney Akers, a resident of that village, who had been somewhat annoyed early that morning by a visit from two gentlemen who told her that they were the "terrible escaped convicts and wanted breakfast."

Grumbling, Mrs. Akers fixed it for them. While the meal was being prepared, the visitors locked her teenage daughter and a neighbor who was in the house in a bedroom to make sure they did not spread the alarm. When their involuntary hostess went to the spring-house to get some milk, Tracy followed her, his rifle cradled in his arms. As they ate breakfast, both men appeared to be agitated and nervous.

"While in middle of the meal," Mrs. Akers said later, "the whistle of the nearby sawmill blew, and they both jumped up like rockets."

During breakfast, they talked a great deal, saying that they did not want to hurt anybody, but if brought to bay the people who betrayed them would suffer for it.

"The country roundabout Monitor was built for the use of escaping convicts," a reporter wrote. "A straggling fir forest, broken here and there by clearings, low hills, deep gullies, and creek bottoms filled with thick undergrowth, afford continuous cover for miles. There is an occasional road to cross, but it is the work of a few seconds to do so, and, again plunged in the wilderness of shrubs and second-growth firs, the fugitive is as safe from detection as if he were walking the streets of Portland."

Spooked by the mill whistle, Tracy and Merrill were soon on their way again, with the pursuit forming behind them. Knowing that if the convicts continued to flee north they would have to cross the deep gorge through which Pudding River flowed, Sheriff Durbin detailed five members of the posse to set up a watch just downstream from the railroad bridge, while he and his men threshed the bushes and drove the outlaws in that direction. Unbeknownst to the sheriff, one of the five men, Jack Luherman, had been an inmate at the Salem prison until recently released, had known Harry Tracy very well, and now revealed an important piece of information.

"See that bend in the road?" he told Major Leabo, the officer in charge of the unit. "Just beyond it is a house owned by a woman named Mrs. Koonz. She's Tracy's sister. Do you suppose he'll pay her a call, since he's in the neighborhood?"

Thinking it likely he would, Major Leabo relayed the information to Sheriff Durbin, who, with the militiamen, the bloodhounds, and the various posses, were working their way down Pudding River, suggesting that they close in carefully just in case Tracy did show his fraternal affection by looking in on his sister for a few minutes on this lovely June afternoon.

But hardly had the order been given and the khaki uniforms mingled with the greenery of the bluff than "Snap" Arms, a courier of Company "D," came scorching down the pike with the news that the convicts had been seen at Graves' ranch, three miles from Needy.

Alas for well-laid plans!

Though the reliability of the report was doubted at first, it later was confirmed by a farmer named E.D. Graves who said that the outlaws had paid him a call and helped themselves to all the edibles in sight, including a five-pound hunk of bacon. Again, Tracy and Merrill had done the opposite of what they had been expected to do.

POSSE GIVES UP

ALL TRACE OF TRACY AND MERRILL IS LOST

THEIR PURSUERS GO HOME

By Saturday, June 14, the pursuers were getting discouraged, their pessimistic mood deepened when the lead story in the *Oregonian* declared:

> *Tracy and Merrill were not captured today, nor are they likely to be, unless, elated by their success in eluding their multitudinous pursuers, they become too bold and present a target for some reward-hunting potshooter.*
>
> *Where they are no man can say. Since noon Thursday they have gone their way unseen and unheard, save in the imagination of rumor-mongers.*

Getting carried away with his role as a critic of the method and means being used by the law officers who were doing their best to catch up with he fugitives, the unnamed "Special Correspondent" waxed facetious, writing that "Now there is a woman in the case. Her name is Dame Rumor."

Indeed, the lady was deeply involved, as she had been from the beginning. Just as Sheriff Durbin and his fellow officer, Sheriff Cooke, who, from an adjoining county had recently joined him in the chase, were about to disband their posses and send them home, Dame Rumor was heard from again.

The two escaped convicts had taken breakfast at Barlow, a town ten miles to the northeast, at four o'clock that morning, a courier who had ridden frantically to carry the news told Sheriff Cooke. Since the man was known to be reliable, Cooke immediately passed the word on to Sheriff Durbin, who, with Walla Walla prison guard Carson, had just taken the bloodhounds into the creek bottom near the Graves Ranch, where they were trying to pick up a fresh scent. There then ensued a scene that challenged the "Special Correspondent's" writing talents.

> *A man was sent to the edge of the wood to shout for him to return, and he and Carson were the next minute hurrying for the ranch, while the dogs, scenting news in the air, ran joyously on ahead. There was a brief conference, and it was decided to move to Barlow without delay. The cavalcade, consisting of at least 10 vehicles, was ready to proceed in 10 minutes, and, amid the farewells of the people at the ranch, who for the past two days have experienced the most exciting times of their lives, the procession drove off.*
>
> *There was no hesitation this time. Along the road for miles clouds of dust showed where buggies and carryalls were flying along, and in less than an hour the telephone station at Needy was fairly surrounded with rigs, while heavily armed men swarmed and banked thickly around the telephone, awaiting further news. Cooke emerged from the telephone booth with a look of satisfaction on his face. The men, he said, had come into a store at New Era that morning and had been last seen west of the railroad, making for the river.*

At long last, it appeared that the showdown had come.

> *The members of the posse clutched their rifles firmly, and thought about how to use them. The bloodhounds pricked up their drooping ears and looked interested. Everybody climbed into conveyances, and the procession was about to move when Durbin, who had been a little suspicious of the report from the first, suggested that part of the posse remain behind until he and Cooke with the bloodhounds and about six men went to the front to see what could be done.*

This turned out to be the best idea Sheriff Durbin had had since the chase began. Two miles from Barlow, a couple of local citizens came out to meet his group and disgustedly informed them that the rumor was "a fake, pure and simple."

It had originated in a saloon, they said, and had been set afoot by speculation as to how two hobos, who had been seen in the neighborhood of Barlow that morning, could terrorize the country if they chose to tell people they were Tracy and Merrill.

Two oddballs with a weird sense of humor had done just that, appearing in a woodchoppers camp carrying rifles, staying just long enough to tell their story, have breakfast, and then disappear, never revealing their identity.

This time, when Sheriffs Durbin and Cooke disbanded their posses, it was for real, both men vowing that they would pursue the escapees no further unless solid evidence of their whereabouts was given them. In concluding his story the *Oregonian* "Special Correspondent" pronounced his benediction to the chase:

> *Where the convicts are now, no one knows. They may be walking calmly along some country road in Eastern Clackamas County, headed for the mountains; they may be working their way toward Portland with such information as to the country as they can obtain from the people they meet; or they may be sleeping peacefully in the tangled wilderness that covers Rock Creek bottom, near Graves' ranch. They have five pounds of bacon, sufficient to enable them to travel several days without disclosing their whereabouts by applying to any more ranches for food, and they are undoubtedly rested by this time from the strain of the first flight ahead of the hounds. It is more than likely that they will come eventually to Portland, for men of their character are unused to outdoor life, and as soon as they get ready to go to work at their trade, that of holding up people, they will want a city as a field of operations.*

Published in the same issue with the "Posse Gives Up" story were photographs of some of the people involved, along with three unflattering cartoons depicting Sheriffs Durbin and

Cooke and prison Guard Carson. In a crass effort to appeal to the stay-at-home reader who had never joined a posse in his life, the *Oregonian* reporter implied that if *he* had been put in charge of the pursuit, he would have handled it much better.

Perhaps he would have. But he should have quit while he was a winner and refrained from predicting that, being city men, Tracy and Merrill soon would show up in Portland where they could resume their careers as holdup men. Because, as always, they did exactly the opposite of what they were expected to do . . .

Oregon Historical Society

Republicans rally in Salem, in 1902, the year Harry Tracy and David Merrill shot their way out of the state prison.

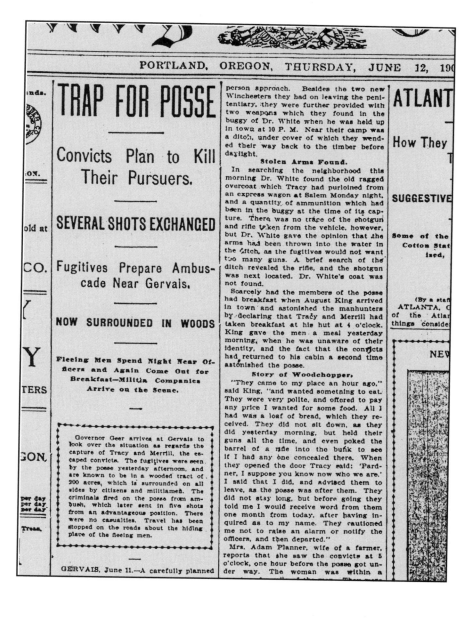

PORTLAND, OREGON, THURSDAY, JUNE 12, 190

TRAP FOR POSSE

Convicts Plan to Kill Their Pursuers.

SEVERAL SHOTS EXCHANGED

Fugitives Prepare Ambuscade Near Gervais.

NOW SURROUNDED IN WOODS

Fleeing Men Spend Night Near Officers and Again Come Out for Breakfast—Militia Companies Arrive on the Scene.

Governor Geer arrives at Gervais to look over the situation as regards the capture of Tracy and Merrill, the escaped convicts. The fugitives were seen by the posse yesterday afternoon, and are known to be in a wooded tract of 200 acres, which is surrounded on all sides by citizens and militiamen. The criminals fired on the posse from ambush, which later sent in five shots from an advantageous position. There were no casualties. Travel has been stopped on the roads about the hiding place of the fleeing men.

GERVAIS, June 11.—A carefully planned

person approach. Besides the two new Winchesters they had on leaving the penitentiary, they were further provided with two weapons which they found in the buggy of Dr. White when he was held up in town at 10 P. M. Near their camp was a ditch, under cover of which they wended their way back to the timber before daylight.

Stolen Arms Found.

In searching the neighborhood this morning Dr. White found the old ragged overcoat which Tracy had purloined from an express wagon at Salem Monday night, and a quantity of ammunition which had been in the buggy at the time of its capture. There was no trace of the shotgun and rifle taken from the vehicle, however, but Dr. White gave the opinion that the arms had been thrown into the water in the ditch, as the fugitives would not want too many guns. A brief search of the ditch revealed the rifle, and the shotgun was next located. Dr. White's coat was not found.

Scarcely had the members of the posse had breakfast when August King came in town and astonished the manhunters by declaring that Tracy and Merrill had taken breakfast at his hut at 4 o'clock. King gave the men a meal yesterday morning, when he was unaware of their identity, and the fact that the convicts had returned to his cabin a second time astonished the posse.

Story of Woodchopper.

"They came to my place an hour ago," said King, "and wanted something to eat. They were very polite, and offered to pay any price I wanted for some food. All I had was a loaf of bread, which they received. They did not sit down, as they did yesterday morning, but held their guns all the time, and even poked the barrel of a rifle into the bunk to see if I had any one concealed there. When they opened the door Tracy said: 'Pardner, I suppose you know now who we are.' I said that I did, and advised them to leave, as the posse was after them. They did not stay long, but before going they told me I would receive word from them one month from today, after having inquired as to my name. They cautioned me not to raise an alarm or notify the officers, and then departed."

Mrs. Adam Planner, wife of a farmer, reports that she saw the convicts at 5 o'clock, one hour before the posse got under way. The woman was within a

ATLANT

How They

SUGGESTIVE

Some of the Cotton Stat ised,

(By a staff ATLANTA, G of the Atlan things conside

NEW

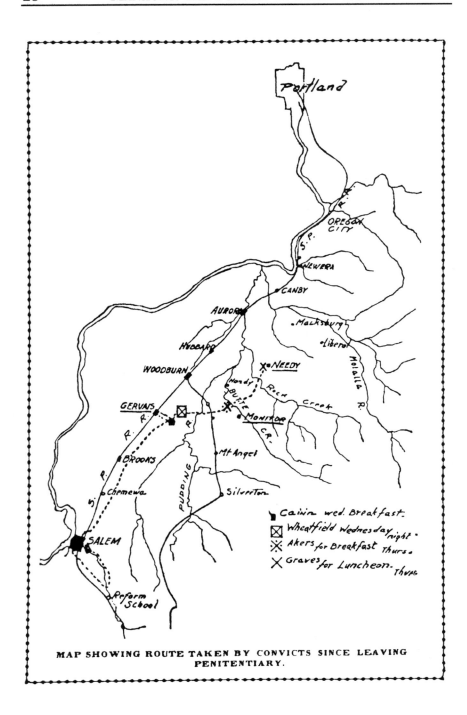

Portland

OREGON CITY

S. P.

NEW ERA

CANBY

AURORA

.Macksburg

.Liberal

Molalla R.

HUBBARD

NEEDY

WOODBURN

Hardy

Rock

Creek

BUTTE

MONITOR

GERVAIS

R.

R.

R.

C.R.

BROOKS

Mt Angel

Chemewa

PUDDING R.

Silverton

SALEM

Reform School

Cabin wed. Breakfast.

Wheatfield Wednesday night.

Akers for Breakfast Thurs.

Graves for Luncheon. Thurs

**MAP SHOWING ROUTE TAKEN BY CONVICTS SINCE LEAVING
PENITENTIARY.**

CHAPTER THREE

ACROSS THE COLUMBIA

A dding the theft of another team of horses to their already long list of crimes, Tracy and Merrill headed not for the city of Portland but north toward the Columbia River. Details of the route taken and the crimes committed by Tracy and Merrill were passed on to the eager reading public by an *Oregonian* reporter.

Around midnight Saturday, two horses had been taken from the barn of W.G. Randall, five miles southeast of Oregon City, hitched to a wagon, and then driven away. The track led across an unguarded Clackamas River bridge, turned off on a road toward Portland, then the two men appeared to have gone on foot to a slough adjacent to but not connected with the Columbia River. A reporter described what happened:

> *George Sunderland and Walter Burlingame were enjoying a quiet boat ride on the placid waters of Columbia Slough about 12:30 o'clock this afternoon, when two gentlemen appeared upon the bank, pointed rifles at them and asked them to come ashore. They had been in the slough about long enough, so they complied, and so grateful were they to their new-found friends for asking them ashore that when the latter called for food it was cheerfully supplied.*

After eating, the two armed men asked to be rowed across the Columbia River. When Burlingame and Sunderland said that the slough was not connected to the river and that the two fugitives would have to traipse overland a mile or so and acquire a boat on the river's south shore, Tracy and Merrill "suggested" it would be helpful if the two men would come along as guides, carrying the thirty-pound sack of ammunition while Tracy and Merrill packed the rifles. Under the circumstances it seemed reasonable to accept this suggestion without argument.

Reaching the river at Fisher's Landing, W.W. Paddock, who had a boat moored there, was added to the party. When it was suggested to him that he help row the group across the river to the Washington shore, he, too, accepted their invitation.

> *It had by this time begun to dawn upon the young men who their new acquaintances were and their suspicions were confirmed by the conversation of the men, who began to ask what had happened since the escape from the Penitentiary.*

Tracy, who sat with his rifle in his lap at one end of the boat, had very little to say during the trip, while Merrill, who was at the other end of the boat, became very talkative.

Among other revelations, Merrill said that while they were hidden in the wheat field near Gervais with the posse closing in, he had drawn a bead on Sheriff Durbin and been about to fire when Tracy discouraged him, arguing such a course would precipitate a battle, which might delay their escape.

"I'm sure we killed Ferrell and Jones," Merrill said, "but I don't know about Tiffany, though I did see him fall."

When told that Guard Tiffany was dead, too, neither man expressed any remorse, saying that if the guards had done what they had been told to do they would not have been shot, but, because they ran or resisted, they got just what they deserved. Tracy finally joined in the conversation.

"I wasn't the least afraid of them bloodhounds," he said. "We fooled them. We didn't intend to kill the guards. I told Jones not to move, but he began to make signals after he had his hands up. Those guards were fools to allow us to climb up that ladder and skin over the walls. We've got about all the money we need and plenty of ammunition."

Lowering their voices, though still speaking loud enough to be overheard, Tracy and Merrill argued briefly about the direction they ought to take after reaching the Washington shore. Their listeners gathered that Tracy favored traveling northeast, to the Yakima country, while Merrill wanted to go north toward the Olympic Peninsula. Before leaving the boat, Merrill said defiantly:

"We're not bad men, but we intend to get away. If anybody stops us, they are going to get hurt. With us, it's a case of burn at the stake or get shot."

On landing, Merrill asked Sunderland for his pocketbook. After it had been produced and examined, Merrill said, "You have a $5 gold piece there, I see, but I won't take it. I'll just take $2. But I ain't a bad sort of fellow, and to show you what I mean, I'll give you this Elk's badge that I got off a fellow the other day (Dr. White)."

Before parting with their ferrymen, Tracy and Merrill shook hands all around, then promised that when they "made a raise" they would send them fifty dollars for their trouble.

Since David Merrill had been born and raised in the Vancouver, Washington, area, he knew this country like the lines in the palm of his hand. Now that the fleeing men were in another state and county, yet another sheriff took charge of organizing posses to pursue them. Three Portland detectives came along as advisors, while reporters from the *Oregonian* continued to cover the story. One of them wrote:

> *The country is much the same as in Oregon, formed of low-lying hills, cut by ravines, and overgrown with underbrush and scrub firs which afford the best kind of cover. As the men are armed with 30-30 rifles and have an abundance of ammunition, it does not seem likely that the desire to capture them will burn any more fiercely in the breasts of their new set of pursuers than it did in those of the posse that laid down its arms and gave up the fight at Barlow Friday afternoon.*

Again the telephone lines became busy, as Sheriff Marsh of Clark County, Constable Tomlinson, and detectives Day, Kerrigan, and Snow of Vancouver were ordered on the case, backed up by Sheriff Cooke of Clackamas County, Oregon, and half a dozen other Oregon law officers who, if they had no legal authority on this side of the river, at least could join the posse as volunteers. By the time they and their weapons and ammunition were all piled into a large carryall pulled by a team of big black horses, the rig was so loaded down that its springs sagged onto its axles.

"The ride was an extremely dusty one," a reporter wrote, "and for the first two miles every buggy was halted to know if its occupants had any tidings of Tracy and Merrill."

None did. But as the posse moved on, one thing after another delayed it. First, a piece of harness broke. The resident of a nearby ranch repaired it with a piece of rope, then "onward went the posse." It occurred to some of the men that they ought to test their rifles, just to make sure they were in shooting order. All were, except one, the rifle and the cartridges turning out to be of different calibers. The mismatch was remedied by sending a posse member to another nearby ranch, where he borrowed a Springfield and suitable ammunition.

"Just wait till I see if this cartridge fits," remarked posse member Goeghan. Slipping in the cartridge with a business-like air, he raised the gun, and the next moment there was a satisfactory bang. "It'll do," Goeghan said. And again the posse was on its way.

Discussing the line of strategy to be followed during the chase, the posse leaders decided that the best thing to do was, "Head the convicts off. Stay in front of them. Meet them as they come on." Trouble was, nobody knew where the two fugitives were, though with all the commotion the pursuers were making the convicts would have no difficulty locating the mob on their trail.

No matter, the posse leaders said. Sooner or later Tracy and Merrill would reveal their presence by stealing a pair of horses or holding up a settler for clothes or food, then the chase could resume at that point.

To aid *Oregonian* readers in keeping up with what was going on, the newspaper began running a weekly notice in the following form:

Convicts' Itinerary

Monday, June 9, 7 A.M.—Left penitentiary.

Monday, June 9, 10 P.M.—Return to Salem.

Tuesday, June 10, 4 A.M.—Arrive at Gervais.

Tuesday, June 10, 9:30 P.M.—At Gervais.

Wednesday, June 11, 10 P.M.—Surrounded at Gervais.

Thursday, June 12, 2 A.M.—Escape from posse.

Thursday, June 12, 7 A.M.—Breakfast at Monitor.

Thursday, June 12, 12 A.M.—Arrive at Needy.

Sunday, June 15, 11 A.M.—Cross the Columbia.

Sunday, June 15, 11 P.M.—Near Fourth Plain, Clark County, Wash.

———

Crimes Committed Since Escape

Murder of three guards.

Murderous assault on fellow-convict.

Theft of team at Salem, horse at Gervais, team at New Era.

With the escapees now in his home state, Penitentiary Guard Carson made a hurried 250-mile train trip east to the prison at Walla Walla, planning to exchange his worn-out bloodhounds for a fresh pair, then return to the chase. But before he could do so, politics intervened. In his absence, National Guard Company "G" was mobilized and assigned the task of guarding remote farmhouses in the area which Tracy and Merrill might be expected to raid for food or clothes. Not surprisingly, they failed to watch the house of a fifty-year-old German farmer named Henry Tiede, who lived four miles northeast of Vancouver, where Tracy and Merrill suddenly appeared at an early hour Monday, June 16, "offed with the old and onned with the new," then demanded breakfast. With a little persuasion, the badly shaken farmer told his story to a reporter later in the day.

Fast asleep at 6:30 that morning in his lonely bachelor quarters deep in the woods, Henry Tiede was wakened by a loud knocking on his door. Not taking the trouble to dress, he unlocked the door and was startled to see two rifles thrust into his face. Dressed in tattered and torn clothing, with a week's growth of beard on their faces, two grim-looking men confronted him.

"Hurry up," said one of the strangers, "we want something to eat."

Guessing his visitors to be the notorious Tracy and Merrill, Tiede said nervously, "Come in, boys, and make yourselves at home."

Entering the cabin, one outlaw looked under the bed and into the closet, while the other made a careful survey of the woods surrounding the house, then came in and said tersely, "It's safe."

After discovering an eight-pound chunk of bacon Tiede had recently bought, one of the men found a frying pan, stirred up the fire in the cookstove, sliced generous helpings of bacon into the pan, and soon had it sizzling.

"We're damned hungry," the outlaw Tiede guessed to be Tracy grunted in surly apology for their lack of manners. "Any guys around your house hunting us?"

"Not that I know of," Tiede answered politely.

"Can you guess who we are?" asked the man Tiede assumed to be Merrill.

"I'd guess you're the boys who escaped from Salem," Tiede answered.

Assuring him that he had guessed right, the two convicts found a loaf of bread, decided that the bacon was done to suit their taste, then sat down and ate a hearty breakfast without asking Henry Tiede to join them.

"Which was all right with me," Tiede told the reporter later. "I wasn't hungry anyway."

After eating their fill, the two men put what was left of the bacon and bread in a sack they were carrying, then helped themselves to Tiede's stock of clothes, stripping to the skin, tossing their tattered garments on the floor, donning fresh underwear, socks, shoes, trousers, shirts, and overalls from his wardrobe, one of them putting on a black slouch hat, the other a brown cloth cap.

"You can have these rags," Merrill said, pointing to the discarded garments on the floor. "We won't be using them anymore."

A later inspection of the clothes left behind showed that one of the discarded items was the coat stolen from Dr. White at Gervais, whose lapel still showed the impress of the Elks badge given to George Sunderland after the fugitives had been rowed across the Columbia River Sunday noon.

Attired in his new suit, Merrill walked over to a table and saw a copy of the *Oregonian* for June 11 lying there. He gave a cry of surprise.

"Why, Harry, here's some reporter put my picture in the paper!"

"Let's see," Tracy said eagerly. Picking up the paper, he studied it critically. "They've put my picture in, too! It ain't bad."

"No, it ain't," Merrill agreed, joining his friend and studying the two pictures as if they were works of art.

Taking a jacknife out of his pocket, Merrill opened it, then carefully cut out the two newspaper photos, giving Tracy his and keeping his own. After looking uneasily at Tiede, the two men moved to a far corner of the room, where they spent several moments discussing their future plans. Tiede heard Merrill mutter, "Follow my way, I say, to the British Columbia line," to which Tracy responded, "Shhh!" as if he did not wish to give away their plans. Finally Merrill said to Tiede,

"We don't want to hurt you, old man, but we've got ourselves to look after, and we don't want you to pipe us off. So to make you keep quiet we're going to tie you up. . ."

Oh, no!" Tiede protested, ""I might lie here helpless for days and starve to death before anybody comes."

"No fear of that," Merrill said, seizing the German and throwing him down on the bed. After Merrill tied Tiede's ankles together, Tracy lashed his hands behind his back, placed a cloth gag in his mouth, and cinched it tight. Gripping their rifles and bags of ammunition and provisions, the two outlaws left the cabin, closing the door behind them. Once outside, they disappeared into the brush as if the earth had swallowed them.

When he was sure his visitors had gone, Tiede wriggled his body up toward the bedpost, where, by butting the knot behind the gag against a sharp edge, he managed to work the gag loose so that he could breathe better. After working nearly an hour on the rope that tied his hands, he got that loose, too, hobbled across the room and found a knife with which he cut his ankles free. Dressing himself in the tattered clothes the outlaws had so thoughtfully left behind, he made his way to a telephone station at the nearby settlement of Orchard, phoned Sheriff Marsh, and told him what had happened.

Later, it transpired that at the time Henry Tiede was being bound and gagged, Sheriff Marsh and the posse were patrolling the roads east of Orchard, thinking that the convicts were still contained within their lines.

"Great was the indignation," a reporter wrote, "when it became known among the posse that their prey had escaped, after making free with Tiede's bacon and clothing."

A bee-line was immediately made by one contingent of pursuers for the timber north of Tiede's cabin. There, tracks were quickly picked up, but for the time being no bloodhounds could be put on the scent, for the expected set of fresh dogs had not yet arrived.

> *In reply to urgent telegraph and telephone messages, Governor McBride sent word that two bloodhounds will leave the Walla Walla Penitentiary and arrive in Portland about 7 o'clock tomorrow morning, with the understanding that if the dogs are successful in running down Tracy and Merrill, the men in charge of them will share in the reward.*   Oregonian

By now, the rewards offered for the two convicts "dead or alive" totaled $6,000, so it was high time the politicians agreed on how the expert trackers involved in the chase would split the loot.

> *It is understood here tonight, that the dogs on the way here are old dogs in the line of tracking criminals—not the dogs recently used in Clackamas and Marion Counties. Sheriff Totten, of Skamania County, arrived here tonight, and will join in the search.*   Oregonian

Meantime, the leaders of the various posses issued a stern warning: "Don't go in behind them. Head them off. Press on toward Salmon Creek between Brush Prairie and Battleground, which is likely the way they're going."

Since no sign of Tracy and Merrill was found all the rest of that day, it was just as likely, a reporter wrote cynically, that the two escapees had gone to ground deep in the woods, where they were sleeping off the effects of their big breakfast. By now, more law enforcement people were joining the pursuit: Deputy Sheriff Skipton; Walter Lyon, private secretary to Oregon Governor Geer; slain Guard Ferrell's brother; and Multnomah County Sheriff Lou Wagner. With all these determined men in the field, meaningful action could be expected at any time. Unfortunately, when the action did occur, Tracy and Merrill were not involved in it.

Suspecting that the convicts would show up in the Salmon Creek area near the small settlement of Battleground, volunteers William Morris and L.D. Seal left Vancouver together to join in the search on their own, taking a dog with them, planning to lie in wait in the brush along the river, ready to do battle with the fleeing convicts when they showed up. Both men were excellent shots, capable of holding their own in a gunbattle with even the most desperate of men.

Early in the afternoon, posse members Deputy Sheriff Skipton, Walter Lyon, Deputy Sheriff Wagner, Guard Ferrell's brother, and several Salem prison guards came prowling into the woods, looking for the fleeing men. The light was poor. Seeing two shadowy figures lying in wait and hiding in the trees, the Salem contingent assumed the pair to be Tracy and Merrill. Asking no questions, the possemen opened fire. Each man of the Salem group triggered at least one shot, it was later determined, so blame for the ensuing accident was hard to fix. But a bullet probably fired by Deputy Sheriff Skipton struck William Morris squarely in his upper right leg.

"Terrified at the volley from the Winchesters," a reporter wrote, "both Morris and Seal held up their hands, Seal waving a handkerchief. Then the truth flashed on the riflemen's minds. They hurried over to Morris and found that he was bleeding and was seriously wounded."

Placed in a buggy and driven to St. Joseph's Hospital in Vancouver, William Morris was put under the care of Dr. Ebert and Dr. Gilchrist, United States Army surgeons skilled at dealing with such wounds. After examining their patient, they said that he would live, though it might be necessary to amputate the leg.

The accident cast such a pall over the posse that all pursuit of Tracy and Merrill was abandoned for the time being, pending the arrival of the bloodhounds and reorganizing the pursuit to make sure such a mishap did not occur again.

"The shooting was an unfortunate accident," Deputy Sheriff Wagner said. "When hunting men like Tracy and Merrill, you can't ask them to hold up their hands and identify themselves, but must shoot on first sight. I consider it lucky that the man was not killed."

As might be expected, criticism of the posse members by the general public was severe.

> *Many people in this county look with derision on the efforts of the officers to capture Merrill and Tracy. Tonight, more than one officer, as he reached town weary and footsore, was greeted with inquiries like this: 'Well, have you caught them yet? When are you goin' to catch them, mister? Ever goin' to do it?'*
>
> *Oregonian*

After the carry-all he was riding in had been stopped several times to answer a flood of what he regarded as silly questions, one disgusted posse member wearily told its driver, "Drive on. Some people don't seem to understand that we are risking our lives every minute we're in this business."

No doubt, they were. But in spite of all assurances to the contrary, the prevailing opinion in the area was that Tracy and Merrill would not be caught this side of Puget Sound. Headlines read:

CONVICTS GO ON

TRACY AND MERRILL MOVING NORTH

BATTLE WITH TWO PURSUERS

By Wednesday, June 17, the manhunt had reached the normally peaceful village of La Center, Washington, fifteen miles north of Vancouver. Tracy and Merrill were not there, an *Oregonian* reporter wrote, adding vaguely, ". . . but they are supposed to be somewhere within a radius of one or two or three miles. Just where they will be tomorrow morning the day only will bring forth."

Having adopted a policy of getting to a point ahead of the fugitives and then meeting them head-on, the law officers and volunteers were quick to respond to an unsubstantiated report that Tracy and Merrill had been seen making their way toward La Center.

> *The whole posse rushed out after them, leaving the little town in a state of unprecedented excitement; but they came back in due time empty-handed.*

Skeptical of the methods of the large, noisy mob of manhunters, two independent individuals, Bert Biesecker and Luther Davidson, followed their own plan of catching the escapees. Employed by the survey department of the Oregon and Washington Railway, Biesecker knew every foot of the local terrain, while Davidson had soldiered in the Philippines.

Working their way through the brush along Salmon Creek, they reasoned that the wanted men would follow the railroad and the creek north, doing their traveling late at night, so special attention should be paid to railroad bridges and roads along the creek. Around eleven o'clock at night, they were watching a spot where the railroad crossed the creek when they saw a pair of shadowy figures emerge from the trees, go down to the creek, kneel, and take drinks of water. Moving forward as silently as they could until they were within thirty yards of the two suspicious-looking men, Biesecker and Davidson conferred in whispers.

"Think it's them?"

"Got to be. All the possemen have gone back to town."

Though the light was too poor for accurate rifle-sighting, Bert Biesecker raised his gun and sent a bullet whizzing at the shadowy figures. Any doubt that they were the two convicts was resolved when his fire was promptly returned with frightening accuracy, the bullet slashing a hole in the left sleeve of his coat. Davidson also fired, as did their opponents, then, with neither party lingering in the vicinity to assess whatever damage had been done, both retreated and sought shelter behind trees.

After hiding in the darkness for half an hour, the manhunters decided there was not enough light to get a satisfactory shot at the convicts, so they cautiously made their way back to the spot where they had parked their horse and buggy before beginning their stalk. Here, to their surprise as they lit a lantern and prepared to drive to town, they found fresh tracks in the road, as if the outlaws had been about to steal the horse and buggy but had been scared away by approaching footsteps.

"They can't be far away," Biesecker whispered to his friend, after hastily blowing out the lantern. "Let's lie in wait for them. They may show their hand."

But the wily Tracy and Merrill were not to be taken in by such a trick. When not a sound came from the midnight stillness of the woods after long minutes of patient waiting, the two men concluded that their quarry was gone, got into the buggy, and prepared to drive back to town.

They were just about to start when *Bang!* came the report of a rifle. The horse squealed and bolted. Hit by a bullet, the poor animal writhed in pain. Next moment he was struck by other bullets from the unseen foe, and tore madly in the direction of the Fourth Plain Road, en route to Vancouver. Considering the roughness of the ground and the speed of the runaway horse, it was a miracle that the buggy did not upset. The horse never stopped until it reached Vancouver about two o'clock in the morning.

Whether the two manhunters holding on for dear life to the sides of the buggy made any attempt to check the runaway horse and return the fire of the outlaws, they did not say. But the horse-sense shown by the stampeding animal clearly indicated that it wanted nothing further to do with their manhunt.

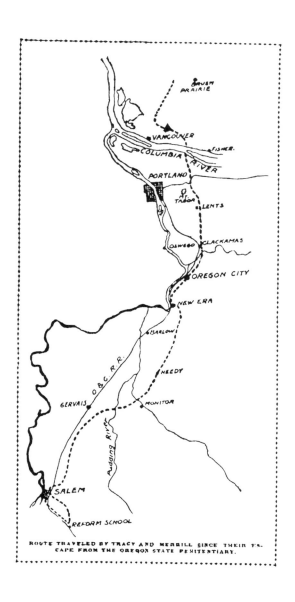

ROUTE TRAVELED BY TRACY AND MERRILL SINCE THEIR ESCAPE FROM THE OREGON STATE PENITENTIARY.

Henry Tiede tells his story.

CHAPTER FOUR

NORTH TO PUGET SOUND

While the authorities were evaluating reports of the latest encounter with the fugitives, the *Oregonian* passed on the good news that William Morris, whose leg had been shattered by a posseman's bullet, was resting as easily as could be expected; there was now hope that the injured leg could be saved.

More intriguing was a letter just received from a woman living in Chicago, who claimed to be Harry Tracy's wife. Addressed to the "Police Judge" in Salem, Oregon, it read:

> *I write you in regard to Harry Tracy. I saw in the Chicago American an item concerning him, which is of no use for me to mention, as you already know the details. The reason of my writing to you is that I am nearly positive, by the picture which was sent, that he is the man whom I was united to in 1893, the 8th day of April.*
>
> *Harry Tracy was in the 'pen' at Little Rock, Ark. on August 14. He got out of there in about nine months. You will enclosed find a small picture of me, but, of course, I expect him to deny ever seeing me, but I will wait patiently to see. I only hope there could be some mistake, but I am afraid there is none. I will close for this time, hoping to hear from you soon. Don't be afraid to tell me all. You will please oblige me. Respectfully,*

MRS. MINNIE TRACY.

P.S.—In the letter which was sent to a gentleman it was stated that Harry Tracy was married to some other person. I hold my marriage certificate, which can be referred to at any time.

When questioned about the letter, Portland Police Chief Gibson said not much was known about Tracy's marital status, but that the letter would be preserved and the lady communicated with "in case Tracy is captured alive."

One problem raised by the letter, the *Oregonian* speculated, was that if Harry Tracy's present age of twenty-five was correct, he could not have been more than sixteen when he married the woman. Of course, lying about his age would not have been considered much of a crime for a man like Tracy, nor would having several wives in several places at the same time trouble him. Only he himself could set the record straight—and for the moment he was granting no interviews.

Meanwhile, the citizens of Vancouver woke up to the exciting news that Biesecker had narrowly escaped being "wounded in a vital part" during a pitched battle with the convicts last night, a happening he at first denied, then admitted, to an inquiring reporter: "They took six or seven shots at me, but did not get me."

Arriving from Walla Walla with his two veteran bloodhounds at eight o'clock in the morning, Guard Carson said neither he nor the dogs had eaten breakfast yet, so he and they were taken to the basement of a nearby hotel and fed, after which he and the dogs posed to have their picture taken for the papers. When the posse assembled for the day's chase, its personnel was duly listed by the *Oregonian*:

At 9 o'clock the start was made; and the various members of the posse tumbled into their carryalls and buggies, clutching their rifles and ammunition. The party included: Sheriff Marsh, Sheriff Totten, Deputy Sheriff Skipton, City Marshal Nerton, and four Portland detectives—Day, Weiner, Snow, and Kerrigan—Walter Lyon, private secretary to Governor

Geer, Constables Tomlinson and Smith, Bert Biesecker,
Luther Davidson, Henry Boardman, and several news-
paper correspondents.

Retracing the route to Salmon Creek taken by Biesecker and Davidson the previous night, just after their battle with the convicts, the possemen let the eager bloodhounds sniff the clothes abandoned by Tracy and Merrill at Henry Tiede's cabin.

"The sagacious brutes immediately began to bay, and at first walked around in a circle. It was a critical moment, and it looked for a few minutes as if the dogs were at a loss, but they at last found a trail leading toward Ridgefield. But Tracy and Merrill were ahead of them, and doing business."

Indeed they were, the business consisting of holding up A. Kauzler, taking the two horses he was driving and mounting them, so that, when the dogs reached that spot, they lost the trail. By this time, it was four o'clock in the afternoon, so the possemen decided the sensible thing to do was go into the village of La Center and have dinner.

The meal was just being served when a messenger hurried in and stated that he had met and recognized Tracy and Merrill about three-quarters of a mile from La Center. Men and hounds immediately started on this new trail, and had not proceeded very far when they heard a number of shots exchanged, but after searching in the brush for a considerable distance, not one single trace of the fugitives could be found.

Tracy and Merrill were "lost" again.

That it was the posse rather than Tracy and Merrill who were lost the reporter tactfully refrained from saying. After holding another council of war, the posse leaders made a decision similar to those it had made before.

"We're too far north now to return to Vancouver," Sheriff Marsh said. "Better camp here tonight and watch the bridges and passes."

Detectives Snow and Kerrigan were sent to guard one bridge five miles away, while Day and Weiner agreed to "defend another bridge against all comers." Other posse members would be guarding various crossroads in the area, the reporter wrote, and would do their best to bar the outlaws' further progress.

"That is the last heard of the posse tonight," the reporter concluded. "It remains to be seen how this famous chase will end."

CHASE GIVEN UP
SEARCH FOR CONVICTS
IS ABANDONED

TRACY AND MERRILL COVER
THEIR TRACKS COMPLETELY

HOUNDS HELD IN READINESS

Sheriff Marsh, deputies, detectives and militia boys have returned to Vancouver, leaving a slim guard to prevent Tracy and Merrill crossing the Lewis River. The outlaws are supposed to be enjoying a gay time on horseback somewhere between La Center and Ridge-field, and changing their boots, to fool the bloodhounds, as often as possible.

The dogs, with Guard Carson, are at Woodland. When a new clew is received, as to the convicts' location the chase will be resumed. It is now up to Sheriff Huntington of Cowlitz County.   Oregonian

"Tired, chagrined, and covered with the dust of many miles of jungle, road and brush," the *Oregonian* of June 18 reported, "Sheriff Marsh, several of his deputies and about a dozen members of Company 'C', Washington National Guard, returned to Vancouver today from an unsuccessful chase after Tracy and Merrill, the escaped convicts. The chase will be resumed when a new clew presents itself."

Admitting that the present whereabouts of the escapees was unknown, Lieutenant Herbert Nunn, in command of a detachment of twelve men of Company "G" of the Washington State National Guard, could say that his men were well armed, should they become engaged in a shootout with the convicts, for their weapons included Winchesters, Krags, Mausers, and Springfield rifles. Furthermore, Lieutenant Nunn was a war-hardened veteran, having fought as a member of the Fourteenth Regiment, United States Infantry, during campaigns in Cuba and the Philippines. Trouble was, he and his battle-ready troops could find nobody to shoot at.

Accompanying an excellent picture of Guard Carson and his bloodhounds, along with a detailed map showing the area over which the chase had been made to date, a newspaper article indicated that Tracy and Merrill were about to receive some aid.

> *Reinforcements are on the way. Ben Merrill, a brother of David, has for some time been employed in one of the lumber camps on Anderson Island. This morning Merrill left camp, saying he was going to the aid of his brother. 'Blood is thicker than water,' he declared, 'and if they take my brother, they have got to take me first.'*
>
> *Mr. Bloom, his employer, argued with him and told him that since he has never been in trouble, he had better keep out of it now. All of his arguments failed, however. Upon leaving the Anderson Island camp, Ben Merrill had about $35 or $45 in cash. It is not known whether he was armed. It is believed he took the boat from the island for Olympia, and will make his way south toward Vancouver, near where the murderers were last reported.*   *Oregonian*

Since Ben Merrill was the brother who opened the bedroom door in his mother's house in Portland to an officer when ordered to do so, thus disclosing David Merrill's hiding place, it seems doubtful that he would have been much help in a shootout. So his statement probably was sheer bravado; at least he was never heard from again.

A peculiarity of the chase that was becoming increasingly evident was that, while the organized forces of the posse seldom got a glimpse of the fugitives, lone, unarmed, harmless individuals not only sighted them frequently but had no difficulty in meeting and talking with them.

A lady schoolteacher riding alone across a meadow a few miles north of Vancouver later reported seeing and waving to them. Though they waved back, they did not pause to exchange small talk.

Mrs. Martin, a farm wife, said they had paid her a call, treating her courteously and politely as they requested and got a piece of bacon and a loaf of bread.

A few minutes after leaving the Martin place, the two outlaws met an itinerant Jewish wagon peddler, with whom they exchanged a few friendly words. When the peddler asked them if they were hunting the convicts, one of them replied:

"No, but you've come about as near as anyone to knowing where to find them."

For the next week, no confirmed sightings of the two fugitives were made, though rumors abounded as to where they had been or appeared to be going. On Sunday morning, June 22, Pat McGuire, whose house was located on a bluff overlooking Lewis River, claimed that during the absence of himself and his family at church, between eight and twelve o'clock, their house had been broken into and a number of articles stolen, including $20 in cash, two pairs of dark-colored trousers, two black hats, two pairs of shoes, about five dozen eggs, and seven or eight pounds of bacon. A hat and a cap were left on the premises, which officers identified as those taken from previous Tracy and Merrill victims.

"The posse is positive that the men have not crossed the river," the *Oregonian* reported, "as the crossings are all closely guarded and all the boats accounted for."

Neither of which precautions had prevented Tracy and Merrill from going where they wanted to go when they wanted to do so before. Nor would they again.

On June 24, Sheriff Marsh received an anonymous letter similar to one received by Sheriff Durbin several weeks earlier. Bearing a Seattle postmark, it reviled Marsh in the foulest of language for his part in the search, stating that the convicts were on the point of leaving Seattle for New Westminster, British Columbia, declaring that they would return December 25, and, as a Christmas present, would kill every person who had participated in the manhunt.

Late that same afternoon, Sheriff Mills, in Olympia seventy-five miles to the north, received a telephone message saying that the fugitives had just been seen in his area . . .

The Sheriff left immediately to join the other members of the posse. The two dogs brought over from Walla Walla a few days ago will now have their first chance to show what they can do. Heretofore they have unfortunately been at too great a distance from the point where the convicts' trail was discovered. They are right on the ground now, and important developments are expected.

Now that the fugitives were well into Washington, volunteer possemen were not as numerous or as eager as they had been in Oregon. "The people of Thurston County do not appear anxious to join the chase and the posse is necessarily small," a *Seattle Post-Intelligencer* reporter noted. "There are not enough men in the posse to adequately guard the roads and woods, and it is feared that this will enable the men to make their escape in the night."

If the *P-I* writer had checked with newsmen on the *Oregonian* staff, he would have learned that even two companies of militia had not been enough to prevent Tracy and Merrill from going where they wanted to go whenever they wanted to go there. But what the posse lacked in numbers it made up for in the determination of two of its members: Charles Ferrell and a man called "Indian Jake." A resident of Reno, Nevada, Charles Ferrell had come to Salem as soon as he learned that his brother, prison guard Frank Ferrell, had been killed during the breakout. Pledging to add $100 of his personal funds to the reward being offered by the State of Oregon for the capture or death of the two outlaws, he swore:

As long as these men are alive, I will be on their trail. I will not be satisfied until I see them pay the penalty for their crimes.

Other than the fact that the man called "Indian Jake" was member of the Cathlamet tribe and lived near Oregon City, nothing was known about his motivation, at first, though more would be learned later. Certainly, he was interested in the reward money, which was said to be in the neighborhood of $6,000. But he, too, was determined to stay with the chase until the bitter end.

After lying low for a week, one of the fugitives made a brief appearance near the hamlet of Bucoda, fifteen miles south of Olympia. Emerging from the woods at an early hour near the residence of Ed Sanford, ". . . a stranger who applied to the house for eggs answered the description of Tracy, Sanford said, for he carried a revolver and appeared to be haggard. He did not venture any information as to his identity and none was requested."

Fifteen minutes later, Guard Carson reached the farmhouse with his bloodhounds, but the dogs, which were young and inexperienced, failed to pick up a scent despite the fact that the tracks left by the armed stranger were plainly visible and easily followed for a distance into the woods.

This inexplicable behavior on the part of the bloodhounds continued to baffle reporters as the chase went on during the next few weeks, just as some of the strange antics of the reporters must have baffled the hard-working dogs.

A day or so later, a *P-I* reporter definitely picked up the scent when he filed a dispatch date-lined July 1:

Alexander Laird's Story

Alexander Laird, residing in a small cabin on the edge of the prairie between Belmore and South Union, came to Olympia and reported to police that yesterday at one o'clock his cabin was visited by a man who claimed to be Tracy, and who bound him hand and foot to his bed and then proceeded to cook a meal. He had a heavy growth of beard, carried a revolver, and his clothes were torn and travel stained.

Laird stated that when the man appeared at his door, he asked for food. Upon entering, he revealed his identity, and said that his companion, Merrill, was guarding the road a distance from the house. Tracy then told the old man that he would be compelled to bind and gag him. He assured him that he was not going to harm him, proceeded to make the old man a prisoner, and then made a raid on the pantry. He remained in the house until five o'clock. About this time, the chimney caught fire, and, fearing that the cabin would be burned, he released Laird from the bed and commanded him to lead the way to the spring nearby for the purpose of carrying water.

They managed to put out the fire, and then Tracy again bound Laird to the bed, and proceeded to utilize things in the cabin to his own benefit. He changed his underwear, took a black coat that belonged to the old man, and also a pair of rubber boots, leaving his old clothes in the cabin. Shortly after six o'clock, he left the cabin, promising Laird that he would leave a note pinned on the gate post of Rancher Johnson's place, three-quarters of a mile down the road, telling Johnson of Laird's predicament so that he could be released. Laird, however, succeeded in releasing himself from the cords, and immediately went over to Johnson's home.

There, Laird learned that a saddle and bridle were missing from Johnson's stable, while a nearby neighbor, John McCloud, had lost two horses. Whether still fearful of Tracy or merely dilatory in doing so, Laird did not report the convict's visit to the office of Sheriff Mills in Olympia until the next afternoon. Visiting Chehalis, twenty-seven miles to the south, at the time, Sheriff Mills was notified of the thefts by phone, but by the time he caught a north-bound train to Olympia, organized a posse, and led it back to Bucoda to pick up the trail the following afternoon, two days had passed and no sign of Tracy and his alleged companion could be found.

The term "alleged" was the applicable word, as matters turned out, for when Harry Tracy next appeared he was still alone.

Meantime, the *Oregonian* reported that less responsible newspapers were publishing rumors that Tracy and Merrill had been flogged while in the Oregon prison, a story vigorously denied by Superintendent J.D. Lee, who stated categorically:

*As an answer to all of them, allow me to say that nei-
ther Tracy nor Merrill was ever struck by a lash of any
kind, whip or rod, not even by a Brockway spanker.*

In a vague accounting of his movements the past two days,
Tracy later said that one of the horses he had stolen had fallen
and broken its leg, so he abandoned it and rode the other one.
Reaching South Bay on the outskirts of Olympia at midnight,
he turned the second horse loose and caught a few hours sleep
in the cemetery, making plans for an early start and a change
in his mode of transportation, next day.

Long famed for the quality of its oysters, the tide flats at the
southern end of Puget Sound near Olympia, Washington, were
lined with a number of camps where the tasty bivalves were
gathered, iced, cooked, or canned. Appearing at the camp of the
Capital City Oyster Company at five o'clock in the morning
Wednesday, July 2, Harry Tracy entered the home of Horatio
Alling, who, with the camp cook, William Adair, was about to
start the working day.

"I'm Tracy," he said curtly, covering them with his rifle. "Fix
me some breakfast."

Giving him no argument, they did so. As the meal was being
prepared, two other employees, Frank Scott and John
Messegee, came into the house. Showing alarm, Tracy waved
them to the other end of the room with his rifle, watching them
warily as he ate. Tied to the salt water dock just outside, the
gasoline launch, *N.&S.*, rocked gently on a slack tide. Gesturing
at it, Tracy asked,

"Can a man cruise around Puget Sound in that boat?"

"Sure," Frank Scott, a crew member, answered. "It's a good
boat."

"Would it take a fellow to Seattle?"

"Easy as pie."

"How long a trip would it be?"

"Well, it's about sixty-five miles. Depending on the tides and
weather conditions, it's a six- to eight-hour cruise."

"Then that's where we're going as soon as I've had breakfast," Tracy said. His cold gray eyes glittered with menace. "You
got any objection to that?"

"No, sir," Scott answered politely. "Are we taking anybody else along?"

"Why should we?"

"Well, I thought you had a partner who escaped—who was traveling with you."

"David Merrill, you mean? Oh, he ain't around anymore. I killed the son-of-a-bitch several days ago."

Finding that chilling statement a real conversation-stopper, Frank Scott asked no more questions. But once breakfast was over, Harry Tracy seemed to feel he should elaborate on the subject. Without relaxing his vigilance in any way, keeping the rifle resting in his lap, he told what had happened to his convict companion.

"Dave Merrill was a no-good coward, who's had it comin' for a long time. First thing that peeved me about him was when I read in the Portland paper how him and his mother got me arrested in the first place. Then after we escaped, he kept bragging about how he'd set it all up through his friends on the outside, when the fact was it was my friends did most of the work. Another thing we argued about was where we wanted to go—the Olympic Peninsula or east of the Cascades. He said maybe we ought to split up. But I had a better idea. Let's fight a duel, I said."

"And you did?"

"Yeah. What we'd do, we agreed, was stand back to back holding our rifles, take ten paces each, then turn and fire. But I didn't trust him. So when I'd taken eight steps, I fired a shot over my shoulder, hit him, and knocked him down. Then I walked over to where he was layin' on the ground, fired another bullet into him, and killed him."

"Where did this happen?" Scott asked.

"Ten or fifteen miles south of here," Tracy said indifferently. "I dragged his carcass back into the bushes and piled some leaves over it, but I didn't bother to bury him. Like I said, he was no good."

Seeing a man and a teen-age boy come out of the cabin of the boat, Tracy asked Scott who they were. When told that the man was Captain A.J. Clark, owner of the boat, while the tall, red-haired fifteen-year-old was his son, Edwin Clark, Tracy ordered

Scott to instruct them to come into the house for breakfast. Later, both father and son related their encounters with Tracy in a slightly different manner.

Captain Clark's Story

When I entered the house at the oyster company's plant, I noticed that a man with a gun immediately backed into a door leading upstairs. I thought the fellows were playing a prank on me and sat down at the table. I and my son Edwin ate our breakfast without thinking of any danger. The rest were sitting in the rear of the room in a strange silence.

After breakfast, I stuck my hands in my coat pockets and started to talk. Suddenly the stranger called out:

'Take your hands out of your pockets, captain. If you have a gun in there, it's no use to pull it.'

I was taken by surprise, and thought the joke had gone too far.

'Who are you?' I demanded.

'Tracy,' he said.

Edwin Clark's story

We had been at work fishing in the oyster beds of Henderson inlet all night when about 6:30 o'clock this morning we were called to shore by the camp cook for breakfast. Entering the house, we saw a stranger sitting in one corner with a gun across his knees and a rather savage expression on his face. We took seats about the table and began eating, the unknown man eating some of the food placed before him, but paying more attention to us than to his meal.

As nothing was said on either side, and the stranger's attitude was rather menacing, matters became uncomfortable. The man in the corner watched us intently. He put his food aside and turned his entire attention to father. Because father kept his hands in his pockets seemed to be the reason for this. Finally he broke the silence by the ejaculation to my father:

'Are you ready to shoot? If you are, I am ready for you.'

Father took the declaration without resentment and returned a laughing reply. This eased the situation. The stranger paid no attention to the reply and interrupted it by a demand for a newspaper. At the same time he said that he was Tracy, and that he had not seen a newspaper since he left the state penitentiary. We doubted that he was the man he claimed to be, but to convince us he ordered us around. At the rate he did this, we soon believed him.

He made the cook put up a lunch for him, while the rest of us made bullet bags for the 300 rounds of cartridges for a revolver. These were shells he had brought with him, but he complained that he had no gun in which to use them.

As we were ready to leave the house, he covered the group with his .30-.30 rifle and ordered us to tie up the cook and one of the other men. This was done by tying their hands behind their backs and then wrapping the rope around their ankles, their legs being bent double at the knees. When this was done, the men were left on their backs.

Captain Clark's Story Resumed

Then he marched us down to the boat and we went on board. He helped us to get the engine started. He sat near the center, where he could watch us all. He always had his gun ready, and it was generally pointing at some of us. He walked up and down the cabin several times, and near the end of the voyage dozed. But when we made the least movement he was awake and alert in an instant.

We left South Point about 10 in the morning. Tracy had told me to steer close to McNeil Island, the Federal prison, so that he could get a shot of one of the guards on the walls, but when I realized he was unfamiliar with these waters, I managed to avoid going close enough to give him a target.

We came north by Nisqually Reach. We passed McNeil about 11 o'clock and Point Defiance at 1:30. When we were off Tacoma, the tug Seafoam *persisted in*

*running toward us. The captain was just fooling a lit-
tle with our party. He is a friend of mine. Tracy, when
he saw that the tug was coming for us, reached for his
gun and placed his finger on the trigger. He wanted to
fire, but I explained that it was a mariner's josh, and
we eventually left the tug behind us. We passed Vashon
Point about 4 o'clock, and from there had a straight run
to Meadow Point.*

*The engines broke down twice, and Tracy helped us
to fix them, but with his gun in one hand. All the way
down the Sound he entertained us with dime novel stories of his deeds and by joshing my son about his red
hair.*

Though Captain Clark wanted the voyage to end as soon as
possible, Tracy said he did not want to reach the spot where he
planned to disembark before darkness fell. Dropping anchor off
Meadow Point, just north of Seattle, at 6:30 p.m. while it was
still broad daylight, the convict remained aboard until dusk fell
an hour later. Before going ashore, Tracy asked Frank Scott,
with whom he had become quite friendly, if he knew this area
well.

"Yes, sir. I do."

"Could you guide me inland on a trail that would take me to
Lake Washington?"

"Sure, I could do that."

"Good. Some friends are meeting me there. If you play honest with me and put me on the right trail, I'll turn you loose and
do you no harm. But before we get off the boat, we'll have to tie
up the others so they won't give me away."

Before going ashore, Tracy made Scott tie up Captain Clark
and crewman John Messegee by tightly binding their wrists
and ankles and doubling back their knees, but when he noticed
that the boy, Edwin, had a sore wrist, insisted that he be bound
at the elbows.

"I'll send you a lot of money to make up for kidnapping you
and the launch," he told Captain Clark before going over the
side, "for I'll have a lot of dough pretty soon now. And I won't

forget you other fellows. You've acted pretty decent by me. Well, so long."

Whether Tracy had any previous knowledge of the terrain around Meadow Point is not known, but it is certain he could have picked no locality better suited to his needs. On the shore of Puget Sound two miles north of Ballard, a suburb of Seattle, high, precipitous bluffs rose from the water's edge, while inland the slopes were covered with thick brush. Scattered along the beach were several usually deserted shacks, though from time to time they became temporary shelters for hobos, smugglers, illegal Chinese coming ashore from tramp freighters, and other transients whose business was nobody's business but their own.

Making Frank Scott walk ahead of him as the obliging crew member guided him along a trail leading to the west shore of Lake Washington, Tracy saw what appeared to be a policeman, who probably was carrying a revolver he coveted, approaching.

"Stand aside!" he ordered Scott. "I'm going to hold him up."

"For God's sake, please don't!" Scott pleaded. "You'll implicate me!"

Tracy hesitated, then muttered, "Damn it, I don't want to get you in trouble. I'll wait till you leave me."

Holding the rifle against his side so that it could not be seen as the two men passed the patrolman with a casual nod of greeting, Tracy walked on into Ballard with Scott, then, when they reached the center of town, said he was tired and wanted to rest. Feeling that Tracy was in a mellow mood, Frank Scott risked asking a question that had been on his mind all day.

"You say you killed Merrill?"

"Damn right I did. Like I told you before, he had it coming."

"There's a reward for his capture, dead or alive. If I knew where his body was and told the state of Oregon, maybe I could get it."

"Hell, Frank, they'd screw you out of it."

"Oh, I don't think so. I wouldn't let them know where the body was until they gave me an ironclad promise in writing that I'd get the reward."

"You know, that ain't such a bad idea," Tracy said with a chuckle. "The notion that Merrill is worth more dead than alive appeals to me. Okay, listen close. Here's where you'll find the body . . ."

Later, Frank Scott would tell a wire-service reporter that the instructions given him by Harry Tracy had been so exact that he was sure he could go right to the remains, once the State of Oregon gave him a written promise that the reward money would be his. After completing his description of where he had left the body, Tracy got up and said abruptly,

"You can go back to the boat now."

"What are you going to do?"

"First, I have to get a six-shooter. I need one badly. I must have it. I'll hold up a policeman and get his gun. Then I'll go out to Lake Washington and come down to Seattle by Pike Street."

"What then?"

"Oh, I'll probably hold up Clancy's Saloon and Gambling House. I hear they've got a lot of dough there."

"Since it's the liveliest place in town, they probably have. But holding it up sounds mighty dangerous to me."

"Don't worry about that, buddy. In Seattle, I'm among friends. They can't catch me in Seattle. If they do take me, they will have to shoot me from behind, for no man can kill me from the front."

With that, Frank Scott told a reporter later, Harry Tracy said goodbye, shook his hand, and walked off down the street with his rifle in one hand and his pack over his shoulder.

"While I was mortally afraid of him," Scott admitted, "yet he made a fellow feel at home."

After Tracy left him, Scott hurried back to Meadow Point and went aboard the launch, where he was as surprised to find that Captain Clark and his crew had managed to release themselves as they were to learn that Tracy had turned him loose unharmed. By the time the party reached the city and notified the authorities of Tracy's presence in the area, it was almost midnight.

Though a posse was organized and a search begun as soon as possible, no trace of the escaped convict was found until afternoon, the next day, when Tracy revealed himself in a sensational manner . . .

CONVICT HARRY TRACY LANDS NEAR SEATTLE

Appropriates a Gasoline Launch at South Bay, Near Olympia, Forces Four Men Into Service, and Effects a Landing at Meadow Point, Just North of Ballard

HARRY TRACY, the Oregon convict, who has succcessfully eluded numerous posses since his escape from prison, is either in Seattle or the immediate vicinity.

With characteristic daring he took possession of a gasoline launch belonging to a Seattle man at South Bay, near Olympia, forced four men who had the craft in charge to navigate it to Meadow Point, some two miles north of Ballard, where Tracy disembarked, and his shanghaied crew came on to Seattle to tell the story of their thrilling experience with the convict.

Before making the trip in the launch Tracy had provided himself with food and clothing at the expense of a man living near Olympia, and among his other feats forced six men to line up against a wall while he bound two and took the remaining four to assist him in reaching Seattle.

Tracy told the men he had killed Morrill, his companion in crime, but that story is not credited.

A posse under command of Deputy Sheriff Williams left Seattle early this morning to seek the daring convict.

TRACY, the escaped Oregon convict, is ... in Seattle. He landed last night at ... had a thin sole. Scott took a coat and vest belonging to Alling, and the cook's ...

OLYMPIA, July 2.—(Special)—Will ...

PORTLAND, OREGON, THURSDAY, JUL...

TRACY ON WATER

Steals a Launch and Sails Away.

MAKES WAY TO SEATTLE

Four Men Made to Accompany Him at Point of Gun.

DID TRACY KILL MERRILL?

Convict Says He Did—Making His Way to Boat, to Escape—Robs Right and Left and Binds Several Men.

SEATTLE, July 2.—Harry Tracy, the escaped convict from the Oregon State Penitentiary, arrived in Seattle late tonight in a launch stolen by him at Olympia. He impressed a crew of four men at the point of a rifle and compelled them to bring him to Meadow Point, just outside the northern boundary line of Seattle. Compelling two of the men to bind first one and another of the boatmen, he aided a third ...

clothes for a suit of Laird's, left his shoes and took a pair of rubber boots, and a reddish-brown coat for a black one. He told Laird that Merrill was two or three miles away.

On learning of Tracy's presence, the posse, which was at work near the town of Roy, was called in and was put at work guarding the roads leading to Mason County. The only hope is that direction is the capture of Merrill. It rained hard last night, and Tracy left a plain trail to this city from Laird's as a result of a specially made plate on the foot of the horse he rode.

Where Tracy Is Headed For.

The belief here is that Tracy will be landed from the launch in Mason County, or may attempt to make British Columbia. Messages have been sent out to head off the boat, but on account of its good start it is feared the daring convict will make good his escape. Little fears are entertained for the safety of the other men in the launch, as Tracy does not show a disposition to harm his victims if they obey his orders.

South Bay, where the launch was stolen, is an inlet of Puget Sound corresponding ...

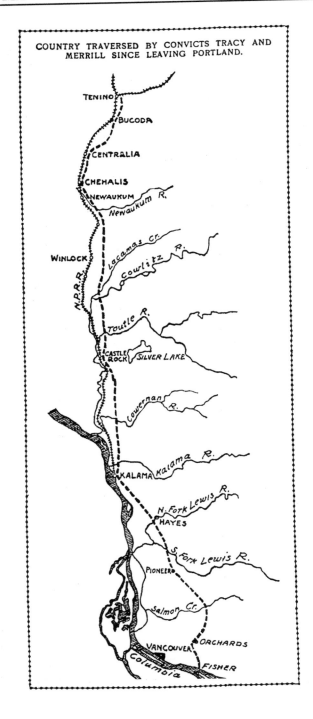

COUNTRY TRAVERSED BY CONVICTS TRACY AND
MERRILL SINCE LEAVING PORTLAND.

CHAPTER FIVE

A RED LETTER DAY

Because of the region's heavy rainfall and thick growth of bushes and trees, a fleeing man need step only ten feet off a road or trail to lose himself in a bewildering maze of cover, where an army of men could not find him. So it was not surprising that, search though the hastily organized posse did, no sign of Harry Tracy appeared until July 3, which newspaper headlines properly called ". . . a red-letter day. . ."

TRACY'S TRAIL OF BLOOD

OREGON CONVICT KILLS TWO
OFFICERS NEAR SEATTLE

GOVERNOR McBRIDE ORDERS
OUT THE STATE MILITIA

Yesterday was a red-letter day in the erratic career of Convict Tracy. He killed Policeman E.E. Breese and wounded fatally Neil Rawley, in the city limits last evening, after having murdered Deputy Sheriff Charles Raymond, of Snohomish County, and probably fatally wounded Deputy Sheriff John Williams, of King County, earlier in the day.

Reconstructing the sequence of events leading up to the killings, it was learned that Harry Tracy and a contingent of possemen had engaged in a shootout the previous day. In mid-afternoon, Deputy Sheriff Raymond, Deputy Sheriff Jack Williams, and Deputy Sheriff L.J. Nelson, accompanied by newspaper reporters Karl Anderson and Louis B. Sefrit, were walking along a railroad track toward Woodinville when they met a man they thought to be a criminal. After questioning him, the officers realized he was not, so turned him loose. Going on down the track toward Seattle until they were a quarter of a mile west of Wayne, they met Deputy Sheriff Brewer, who told them Tracy had just been seen near Wayne. Since this seemed to be an ideal hiding place for a fugitive, they decided to search the area carefully.

Sefrit noticed a path running down to a cabin near the railroad track. It bore the fresh imprint of a man's foot. "This is our place," Raymond said, stepping forward to lead the group toward the cabin.

Rain was falling in torrents. Suddenly from a stump about thirty feet away Tracy's face and neck popped into view, and at the same moment he flung his .30-.30 Winchester into position across the stump, firing point-blank at Anderson. Grazed as the bullet struck the side of his face, Anderson tumbled headlong into the ditch, partly stunned. The cold water revived him, and he was on his feet in an instant. As he rose, Tracy again fired twice, and Raymond, who had just crouched to shoot, reeled back against Anderson, then fell to the ground, stone dead.

Newsman Sefrit, who was armed despite his noncombatant calling, fired at Tracy and missed. Turning his attention to Sefrit, Tracy drove him to the ground with his first shot, then, when the reporter had the bad judgment to shoot again, sent him groveling in the mud with two more shots which singed but did not wound him. From that moment on, Sefrit decided, the only weapon he would carry during the manhunt would be a pencil.

In the meantime, the other newspaperman, Karl Anderson, had plunged into the brush in an attempt to flank Tracy. Meeting Nelson and Brewer, the trio began to move forward, but before they had gone more than a couple of steps, Tracy fired three times at them and a posseman named Williams, who had just joined them. One of the surviving reporters later wrote:

> *Williams crawled out of the brush on his hands and knees with blood apparently streaming from every point. He was shot three times under the heart, and even as he appeared in view lurched to one side and stretched out unconscious. As Williams collapsed, Tracy disappeared. The whole adventure had hardly taken more than two or three minutes.*

Though a newspaper account stated that "Tracy fled through the forest like a hunted animal," his subsequent actions certainly were not those of a timid animal. Encountering a farmer named Johnson driving a wagon toward Bothell a few miles and minutes away, Tracy stepped into the middle of the road and stopped him with an authoritative upraised hand, saying:

"I am a deputy sheriff and one of the men on Tracy's track. I must go to Seattle at once, and need your wagon. You will drive me to the city as quickly as possible; there is no time for delay."

Asking no questions, the farmer obeyed.

In late afternoon, Tracy appeared at the Woodland Park home of Mrs. R.H. Van Horn. Politely, he asked to be fed. Frightened though she was, Mrs. Van Horn said that if he would sit down at the kitchen table and wait for a bit, she would fix him a good meal, so long as he promised not to harm her or a gentleman guest who was visiting her. Saying that he had never hurt a woman in his life and did not intend to start now, Tracy agreed to mind his manners, asking only that she not tell the authorities he had been here until the next morning.

While she was preparing the meal, a knock sounded on the front door. "That's probably the grocery boy," she said, before going to answer it. "He comes around every day about this time to take my order."

"Talk to him, then," Tracy said, moving to a corner of the kitchen where he could not be seen from the front door. "But if you tell him I'm here, you're in trouble."

Opening the door to the grocery boy, Mrs. Van Horn gave him the list she had made out and chatted with him in a normal way to allay Harry Tracy's suspicions. Then, as the boy was about to leave, she took the incredible risk of imperceptibly inclining her head backward toward the kitchen door behind her and silently mouthing the word: *"Tracy!"*

From the way the boy's eyes gleamed, she knew he understood. Whipping the horse pulling the delivery wagon into a dead run, the grocer boy drove pell-mell into the nearby town of Fremont, where he blurted out his news to Sheriff Edward Cudihee, who had just arrived from Bothell to investigate a rumor that Harry Tracy had been seen in the area. As usually happened, "The news of the desperado's proximity to Fremont struck terror into the hearts of bystanders, but a few resolute men quickly resolved to make a desperate attempt to surround the Van Horn home. Patrolman Breese, Neil Rawley, a coal miner, and J.I. Knight, a local insurance man, quickly armed themselves, and headed toward the spot. Sheriff Cudihee also repaired to the place."

In the gathering gloom, Cudihee secreted himself in a spot which gave him an unobstructed view of the team and wagon, which belonged to Mrs. Van Horn's gentleman visitor, parked in front of the house. The three volunteer guards took up positions in a semicircle on the other side of the road. Wary as a wolf, Tracy had two male hostages with him when he came out of the house, the gentleman visitor who had been there when he arrived and an older man who apparently had stopped by after the grocery boy left. Though Sheriff Cudihee and his assistants had been careful to make no noise that would reveal their presence, Tracy must have sensed danger, for, as he approached the wagon, he was carrying his rifle at the ready and was walking between the two men he was forcing to take him where he wanted to go. The insurance man, J.I. Knight, later told a reporter what happened:

> *I was hiding within six feet of the team. Tracy and the men came out, the desperado walking between the two. They approached the horses from the side opposite where I was concealed, and passed within six feet of*

where I was crouching. It had grown dark, so that it was a matter of conjecture as to the exact positions occupied by the three men.

It was then, Knight said, that Breese arose and called out, "Drop that gun, Tracy!" Without an instant's hesitation, Harry Tracy fired two quick shots. By the flash of one, Knight said, he saw Breese fall to the ground.

I did not know at the time that one of the bullets had also found a target in Rawley, who I could see by the flash stood within a few feet of Breese. I am certain that Breese also fired before he fell to the ground. Here I arose from my place of concealment and fired two shots at the retreating murderer.

Sheriff Cudihee was helpless to act, for if he had opened fire he would have risked hitting his own men. As Breese fell to the ground, Cudihee jumped the fence behind which he had been stationed, and fired two shots in quick succession at Tracy, who was fleeing along the road. Later, Cudihee was unable to state positively that he had hit Tracy but was inclined to believe that he did, for he thought he saw the outlaw stumble before he disappeared in the darkness. As soon as the skirmish was over, Cudihee turned his attention to calling an ambulance in which the body of the dead policeman, together with that of Rawley, who was found to be wounded in the right side, could be taken to the hospital as soon as possible.

STATE MILITIA ORDERED OUT

Headquarters National Guard of Washington Seattle, July 3, 1902, 12 M.

Field Orders, No. 1.

Companies B and D, 1st Inf. Regt., N.G.W., will immediately assemble at Armory, in heavy marching order, equipped with forty rounds ammunition per man, there to await further order. Col. Geo. B. Lamping will command detachment of regiment.

By order of commander-in-chief.
JAMES A. DRAIN
Adjutant General.

$5,600 OFFERED FOR TRACY'S CAPTURE

Gov. McBride last evening announced that the state of Washington will pay $2,500 for the capture of Tracy, dead or alive, which with other rewards offered makes $5,600 upon the head of the desperado. The state of Oregon will pay $3,000 for Tracy's capture, making $5,500 offered in the two states, and in addition a brother of one of the guards killed at the Salem peniten-
when the convicts escaped, will pay $100.

Gov. McBride made the announcement for the reward last night at the sheriff's office through his private secretary, J. Howard Watson.

As word of the killings spread next day, the streets in front of the *Post-Intelligencer* building, where bulletins were posted in the windows, were crowded with men, women, and children pushing and hauling at one another in an effort to get a better view.

"It has been many a day," a reporter wrote, "since such excitement prevailed on the streets of Seattle as was the case yesterday afternoon and last night. When the news flashed over the wires that the now thoroughly aroused and reckless murderer had captured a team and was heading for Seattle, men looked at each other with apprehension in their eyes and rushed to the hardware stores to get rifles to join in the man hunt."

Ample evidence was soon forthcoming that neither King County Sheriff Edward Cudihee, nor Deputy Sheriff James Corcoran, who were in charge of organizing the pursuit, were particularly happy with the quantity or the quality of the proffered help.

"Men in all walks of life were anxious to go," a reporter wrote. "Men and boys who would not know how to work the levers of a repeating rifle, were right up in front, pushing their claims to be allowed to join the posse."

But Sheriff Cudihee, a veteran law officer who had first worn the badge in the wild and woolly mining towns of Colorado, disliked amateurs horning into his game, so was not stampeded into accepting unqualified men.

"No man was given a gun unless he was properly identified to the deputy in charge," a reporter wrote. "Every man was impressed with the danger of the undertaking, and the men who are expected to do the best work had the least to say. All they asked for was a repeating rifle and a pocket full of cartridges, and they were ready for anything."

Though the National Guard had been alerted, Governor McBride said that moving the troops assembled at the armory into the field would require a formal request from Sheriff Cudihee. This, the sheriff declined to make, stating bluntly:

"I did not ask the Governor to call out the militia, because I did not think the soldiers would be of any use in a hunt like this."

After a long day and night of pursuing Tracy, exchanging gunfire with him, seeing two officers killed and a third probably mortally wounded, Sheriff Cudihee was not inclined to speak diplomatically to the press upon his return home at 1:30 in the morning, wet, weary, his trousers torn and a hand badly cut by running into a barbed wire fence.

"There are too many men after Tracy," he said bitterly. "Twice today we had him dead to rights, then other men butted in and we lost him. I had him just as certain as fate had not Breese and Rawley come up at the Van Horn's house. I told Breese not to come up there, as I wanted to ambush Tracy myself and make sure.

"I made up my mind to shoot the man who carried a gun out of that house. I did not propose to take any chances and wanted to make sure of my man. I had a perfect view from three sides and he could not get to his horses without my seeing him.

Then the shooting began, and the next thing I knew Tracy came jumping over the fence and I began pumping lead after him.

"I don't suppose I was closer than 100 yards to him when I shot, and it was quite dark. Had those men stayed away I would have had a beautiful chance to bring him down. The same thing was true at Bothell, when that old man came crowding in with his horse, which Tracy took away from him."

PORTLAND, OREGON, FRIDAY, JULY 4, 19

TRACY'S TRAIL OF BLOOD

Oregon Convict Kills Two Officers Near Seattle.

WOUNDS OTHER MEN IN POSSE, ONE BADLY

Desperado Engages in Two Hot Battles and Continues His Wild Flight.

GOVERNOR M'BRIDE ORDERS OUT THE STATE MILITIA

Also Offers a Reward of $2500 for Fugitive—Tracy Makes His Way Back to Seattle, and Men of All Walks in Life Join in the Chase.

SEATTLE, July 4.—Yesterday was a red-letter day in the erratic career of Convict Tracy. He killed Policeman E. E. Breese and wounded fatally Nell Rawley, in the city limits last evening, after having murdered Deputy Sheriff Charles Raymond, of Snohomish County, and probably fatally wounded Deputy Sheriff John Williams, of King County, earlier in the day. In his hopeless flight for safety yesterday, at no consideration for human life, Tracy has covered probably 60 miles. He was first encountered by a Seattle posse near Bothell at 3:30 o'clock yesterday afternoon. Evidently, the convict saw his pursuers before they saw him. He had taken a commanding position in a clump of huge firs, and opened fire before he was discovered. He fired five shots in all. Raymond was instantly killed by one of the Winchester rifle balls. Another struck the raised rifle held by Williams, split in four parts, and entered the

himself in a spot which would command an unobstructed view of the team hitched in front of the Vanhorn home, and the three other volunteer guards took up positions in a semicircular fashion on the opposite side of the road. Neither had to wait long, for hardly had the men secreted themselves than Tracy, walking midway between an aged rancher, who he had held up at the point of his gun and forced to drive him towards Fremont, and another man, who mysteriously disappeared after the shooting, left the house from the front door.

Story of Man in Battle.

What followed is best told in the words of Mr. Knight, who participated in the thrilling encounter, which immediately followed. He said:

"We got the boy to direct us to the house," said he, "and stationed ourselves as described. We readily located the spot by the fact that the team was hitched in

They the
Seattle fr
quarter d
met Dep
back to
had been
back on
entered a
Here the
as it was
Befrit r
a cabin
the fresh
is our pl
forward.
Nelson a
of the ca
west.

Trac
The me
their rifl
The rain
Suddenly
Tracy's f
at the s
Winchest
stump.
taneously
fired poi
grazing h
long int
cold wat
and he w
he rose

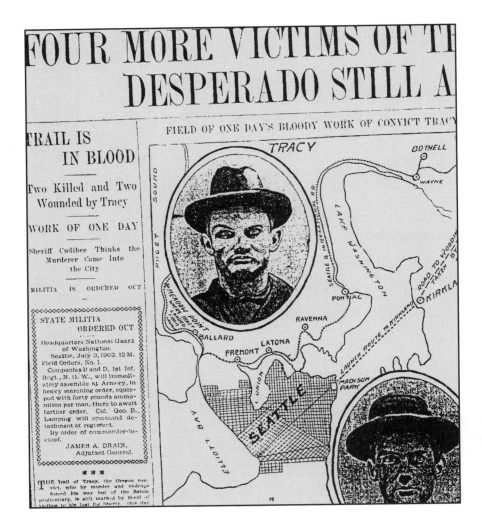

CHAPTER SIX

EDWARD CUDIHEE —MANHUNTER

A bulldog of a man, King County Sheriff Edward Cudihee took the murder of his deputies so personally that he vowed he would not give up the chase until Harry Tracy was captured or dead, no matter how far the trail might lead outside his jurisdiction. This was vital to the continuity of the pursuit, for at that time murder was not a federal crime and United States marshals were not authorized to follow a killer within the boundaries of a state, though they could do so within a territory. This meant that once a murderer moved out of one county and into another, an entirely new set of officers had to take up the chase.

It was an indication of the tenacity of Sheriff Cudihee that, after a long day on Tracy's trail, he did not return to Seattle until 1:30 the next morning, leaving on watch a large number of deputies, who would be relieved in the morning by carefully screened volunteer possemen. When the replacements did arrive, they found Sheriff Cudihee already back on the job.

Meantime, down in the Olympia area, law officers admitted that they were "up in the air" so far as the whereabouts of Tracy's partner-in-crime, David Merrill, was concerned. Sheriff Mills said that not the slightest trace of him had come to light, and that, after having been on the chase for a week, he had no authentic information as to Tracy and Merrill being together north of the Cowlitz country.

"At several places where Tracy secured provisions," Sheriff

Mills said, "he stated that Merrill was close by, but Merrill was not actually seen. The search for Merrill has practically been abandoned so far as Thurston County is concerned."

Whether Frank Scott, crew member of the steam launch that had carried Harry Tracy from Olympia to Seattle, had told Sheriff Mills about the gun duel and not been believed, is unclear. Certainly, he was not hesitant about telling it to a representative of the Associated Press.

"No more oyster-fishing for me," he gloated exuberantly. "After this week I will be living in luxury at the expense of the taxpayers of Oregon."

So confident was Scott of the truth of the story Tracy had told him, that he was throwing up his job in Olympia and going to Chehalis a few miles to the south, where he was sure the "minute details" Tracy had given him would lead him to the body. Once located, he would report it to the authorities, then receive the reward being offered for it "dead or alive" by the State of Oregon, which he understood to be at least $6,000.

Two column-inches below his newspaper story, was another, datelined Boise, Idaho, 500 miles to the southeast, which read:

> *A man in Nampa is held on a charge of vagrancy, whom the officers believe to be David Merrill, the convict, who escaped from the Oregon penitentiary with Tracy. He was arrested this evening, and the officers are in communication with the Oregon officers respecting him.*

Dame Rumor was in the saddle again . . .

NO SIGN OF TRACY
DRIVES AWAY WITH STOLEN
HORSE AND BUGGY

NEIL RAWLEY,
WOUNDED, DEAD

Where Convict Harry Tracy is no one knows. He has again made his way out of a country teeming with armed men, and when last seen was going north with a stolen horse and buggy. Sheriff Cudihee, of King County, now proposes to station parties of three to seven men all over the county.

Neil Rawley, who was wounded in the battle near Fremont Thursday, is dead. Deputy Sheriff Williams, who was wounded in the fight near Bothell, has a good chance of recovery.

On July 5, newspapers reported that on roads patrolled by guards armed with new Winchester rifles, Harry Tracy, the Oregon convict still was eluding capture.

His whereabouts in a district of 20 miles radius are absolutely unknown. Sheriff Cudihee's office has been deluged with reports of his appearances. Each was traced down to its source by posses. All were groundless."

Neil Rawley died of wounds suffered in the gunfight in which Policeman Breese was killed, while Deputy Sheriff Williams, though seriously wounded, still clung to life. Up to this time, Tracy had killed three men in the Seattle area, all so popular that their murders incited hundreds of friends to volunteer their services in hunting down the desperado. Asked to donate guns to posse members, one hardware store gave away its entire stock of firearms in a few hours.

Around one o'clock in the morning, July 5, a man thought to be Tracy appeared outside a house on the outskirts of Ballard, defiantly shouted his name to the sleeping occupants, then coolly hitched a horse to a buggy and drove off in the direction of Seattle.

Posses were called in, picketing in a circle around the neighborhood where he was supposed to be. Believing that Tracy had eluded them by some divergent path leading to Lake Washington, Sheriff Cudihee called in the greater part of his deputies and their volunteer helpers, pulling them back toward Seattle and establishing a cordon of pickets along the entire road.

"We really can't state positively where Tracy is," the sheriff said. "We are watching closely for his next appearance. We are not sure he is near Bothell. The reports received, however, make it imperative that we should patrol this part of the county with increased vigilance. We can take no chances. Nearly 50 men are tonight on watch all the way from Woodland Park to Woodinville. We should get some trace of him tomorrow. If we do, the posse will be hard on his track."

Because rain had fallen steadily for the past three days and nights, the only thing the possemen could be sure of was that Harry Tracy was getting very wet unless he had found shelter in one of the many empty shacks in the area or had managed to slip through the cordon of guards trying to contain him and sought refuge under the roof of a house belonging to a confederate or friend, several of whom were rumored to live in the area.

A woman who lived half a mile north of the Van Horn residence told posse member W.H. Buttner and an Oregon penitentiary guard that she had seen Tracy running through her garden.

"The man you gentlemen are looking for ran through that field less than a half hour since," she said, indicating an open space just north of her house.

"How do you know it was him?" the guard asked.

"He looked just like the picture published in the newspapers," the woman said firmly. "He carried a Winchester rifle in the hollow of his arm. He wore no hat. Wound around his right hand and wrist was a dirty white cloth or handkerchief. He wore a black coat and vest. I don't remember the color of his trousers."

If the two posse members had given as much thought to their pursuit of the outlaw as the lady had to her description of him, they might have had some chance of catching up with him. But their subsequent actions were poorly planned, to say the least. Convinced that Tracy was taking a circuitous route to reach another part of the county road further north, Buttner and the guard started running up the road, continuing in precipitous haste for some distance. Believing that they had gained a lead on their quarry, the two manhunters dropped into a thick hedge of willow trees and waited for Tracy to show up.

"We waited until certain that our man had taken another direction," Buttner said. "Then we proceeded up the road, fearing that we had not gone far enough. We reached Johnson's farm, and stopped to question the man for any information he might have. The guard, believing we had gone too far north, determined to return on the road. I differed with him. We separated and walked in opposite directions."

No sign of Tracy was found by the prison guard during his walk south. But posseman Buttner, in his walk north, *did* find a man who had seen—or *thought* he had seen—a person who *may* have been Tracy.

"I walked up to a sawmill, about four miles north of where we had talked to the woman," Buttner said. "I talked to the foreman, who had been on watch constantly. He knew no late news of the fugitive. He claimed to have seen Tracy pass the mill on the county road in a buggy last night, and started to shoot him.

"He dropped his rifle on the pleading of his wife. She feared he was mistaken in the man. The foreman is now confident that it was the convict, however, because the man would have had to pass the mill on his way to Fremont. The foreman said Tracy held a rifle ready to shoot, glancing furtively into the brush and at the corners of every possible hiding place along the highway."

Whether the foreman's wife should have been credited with saving Tracy's life, that of her husband, or both, must forever remain in the realm of speculation. Certainly, if the shadowy figure in the buggy *had* been Tracy, and if the sawmill foreman *had* fired and missed, the odds were good that Tracy, a good shot in any kind of light, would have returned the fire with deadly effect—and the lady would have become a widow rather than her husband becoming a hero. But nothing happened; so the chase went on.

Meanwhile, Sheriff Cudihee informed Governor McBride that he had all the possemen he could use, so General Drain told the two companies of militiamen that had been standing by in the armory in full battle gear for twenty hours they could go home. Again, the newspapers published an up-to date box score:

Men Killed by Tracy
During and Since His Escape.

Guard Frank B. Ferrell, Salem, Or., June 9.
Guard S.R.T. Jones, Salem, Or., June 9.
Guard B.F. Tiffany, Salem, Or., June 9.
Deputy Sheriff Charles Raymond, Bothell,
   Wash., July 3.
Policeman E.E. Breese, Seattle, July 3.
Deputy Game Warden Neil Rawley, Seattle,
   wounded July 3, died July 4.

As a tragic footnote to the story, Coroner Hoy, who was present at the autopsy performed on Neil Rawley, announced that the .38-caliber bullet found in the body had come from a revolver, not a rifle, and that in all probability the fatal shot had been fired by a posseman, rather than by Harry Tracy.

A news item from Boise, Idaho, stated that the man being held in Nampa on suspicion of being David Merrill had been released, after it was clearly shown that, while he resembled the still-missing man, he was not the person wanted.

For the next few days, all the Tracy stories appearing in the newspapers were of the negative variety, such as the one published in the *Oregonian* Sunday, July 6:

> *Tracy, the escaped Oregon convict, did not come out in the open yesterday, or, at least, no report of his appearance was received. Officers believe they have him surrounded near Bothell, and are playing a waiting game. Tracy's complete outfit was found in the cabin at Bothell where he had his first fight with the posse, which gives rise to the suspicion that his friends have come to his rescue. Some insist, however, that the Bothell officers did not search the cabin very thoroughly after Tracy left it.*

Speculating that the convict-murderer must be somewhere within a circle fifteen miles in circumference, the reporter made a statement not justified by past experience:

Unless the convict stole through the lines last night, he can hardly escape without a battle. Every bridge and crossing, every place of strategic importance in a pursuit of this kind, is guarded by men lying in ambush. Others are patrolling the country.

Adding an element of mystery to the story was the fact that a buggy showing three lights had been seen on a country road a little after midnight near a cabin in which Tracy apparently had changed his clothes.

The buggy was seen by Deputy Sheriff Frank P. Brewer and Deputy Sheriff Woolery, who were spending the cool, rainy night lying in wait near the small village of Wayne. Hearing the buggy approach, they saw its dim outline as it passed, then heard a man say, "This is the town of Wayne."

Immediately following that statement, the two watchers thought they heard a woman's voice reply, but could not make out what she said. When the buggy appeared, they said, it had three lights, one being strung under the front axle. Two of the lights disappeared when the buggy stopped at the cabin where it later was learned Tracy changed his clothes, then, in a few minutes, turned around and again passed the two deputies. As it passed, Brewer called out,

"What time is it?"

"Half past twelve," the man driving the buggy replied without slowing down, then the buggy disappeared into the darkness.

Later, the two deputies explained that they thought its occupant was a young man driving his sweetheart home.

"I couldn't see how many people were in the buggy," Brewer said. "It was pitch dark, and the vehicle went past rapidly."

Causing a bit of controversy afterwards was the fact that the first group of deputies who had searched the cabin near Bothell had found nothing to indicate that Tracy had been there, while the second group, which included Sheriff Cudihee and Deputy Sheriff Nelson of King County, as well as Deputy Sheriff John McClellan of Thurston County, found plentiful evidence that he had.

"McClellan's examination was exhaustive," a reporter wrote.

"He found Tracy's blanket spread in one corner of the loft, with some hay for a pillow. Bread, fresh veal, bacon, butter, a frying pan, a can of salmon put up in Tacoma, and a whetstone for a razor composed the outfit. Both McClellan and Nelson maintain that the outfit was there when the Bothell deputies searched. The loft is well lighted, and they were unable to see how the outfit was overlooked."

Next day, the mystery became moot when Tracy again changed his clothes—this time in the presence of a rancher named Fisher, whose home near Pontiac he briefly visited before taking another country road in the Bothell area. Getting the first-hand details of Tracy's visit from the badly shaken rancher and his not-so-frightened wife, a *Post-Intelligencer* reporter wrote the following story under the headlines:

TRACY CHANGES HIS CLOTHING

Appears at a Ranch House and Secures Food

Talks of His Deeds and Explains His Method of Shooting Men at Close Range

Harry Tracy, the escaped Salem convict, seems to have the cunning of a fox as well as the ferocity of a tiger. While the members of the various posses in search of him were scouring the country for miles, he slipped through the cordon without detection after leaving Fremont Thursday night, and at 7 o'clock Friday morning appeared at the home of August Fisher, a rancher living three and one-half miles north of Ravenna, near Maple Leaf. He ate a hearty meal and exchanged his rain-soaked garments. When he left, he took away with him enough food to last him three days.

As he departed, he told Fisher that he intended to remain in the neighborhood for some time, and that if within forty-eight hours anybody was informed he had been at the house, he would return and kill the whole family. Mrs. Fisher, whom the authorities term a nervy little woman, looked for an opportunity to slip poison into his food, but was watched too closely to carry out her purpose.

Tracy Makes Appearance

When Tracy made his appearance, Fisher was working in a small vegetable garden, and his 15-year-old son Paul was standing near the back porch. The convict carried his gun across his left arm, in a position where it could quickly be brought to bear on any object. He called to Fisher, and when the rancher came to him in response to his summons, told him he wanted something to eat.

"I am Tracy," he said, "and I want you to get me something to eat, and to do it quick. I am hungry as a bear. Both of you must come inside the house with me, and if you make any movement that looks as if you mean injury, I'll kill you."

Fisher admits he was so badly scared he could hardly stand. He and his son preceded Tracy into the house, where Mrs. Fisher and three young daughters were still lingering around the breakfast table. The fugitive told Fisher to ask his wife to get him something to eat as soon as possible. She started to fry some eggs and bacon, and while she was busied with this work Tracy asked Fisher for a pair of dry socks. The rancher replied that the only ones he had besides those he was wearing were hanging on the clothesline, wet from the rain. Tracy then removed his socks and hung them on the back of a chair, near the stove.

Taking Fisher into a bedroom, which opens off the kitchen, he said he would like a suit of clothes. He looked at the masculine apparel hanging on the wall and selected a dark blue sack coat, a pair of corduroy trousers, a black shirt with white stripes and a black and brown checkered patterned cap with a flap which draws down over the ears and back of the head.

"I would prefer the black hat you have there," he remarked, indicating with his hand one that hung on

the wall near the head of the bed, "but I guess it is a Sunday article, and as you appear to be a poor man I will leave it."

While he changed the clothing, he sat on the edge of the bed, with his rifle between his knees. He made Fisher stand in a far corner of the room, and in taking off his wet shirt and putting on the dry one acted with lightning-like rapidity. Just as he pulled on the corduroy trousers, a sudden thought came to him, and he said:

"Fisher, go into the kitchen and tell your wife that if anybody appears down that road, or from any other direction, she and the girls must stand in the doorway. Nobody must come into this house while I am here."

Mrs. Fisher is unable to speak English, this being the reason why the convict did not address her directly. He sat in such a position while he was changing his clothing that he could watch every move she made, however, and was distrustful also of the son, whom he commanded to take a chair and remain quiet until he came out of the bedroom.

While eating the meal, Tracy faced the door and kept his rifle across his knees. He ate ravenously, and after clearing his plate asked for some hot cakes, which were cooked for him by Mrs. Fisher. After the meal, he put on his socks and asked Fisher for a pair of shoes. None suited him until a pair of heavy logging shoes, the kind which lace up the calf of the leg almost to the knee, were brought out. He gave an exclamation of satisfaction on seeing these shoes and asked to whom they belonged, Fisher or his son. He was told they belonged to the boy, and then inquired their size, learning them to be No. 9's.

Maintains Good Humor

"Well, young fellow," he remarked with a grin, as he held up the shoes in order to survey them closely, "you're a husky lad for your age, but those shoes are big enough for most men. You must have come from Maine. The best I have done yet is to wear a No. 8. However, these *will do. I've got to have a new pair anyhow, because these cursed man-hunters are all the time following me with dogs and I must throw them off the track. I'm not afraid of men—I can stand them off, all right—but I don't like the dogs a little bit."*

Several times while Tracy was at the house he mentioned that he was being pursued by dogs and evidenced fear when a dog belonging to a rancher living a quarter of a mile away barked, involuntarily rising to his feet and gripping his rifle. When informed that the dog belonged to a neighbor named Olin, he sat down and resumed his eating.

The convict carried a large revolver with a yellowish maple handle. It was stuck in the band of his trousers, and several times he changed its position slightly after putting on the corduroy trousers. He carried his rifle cartridges in a small buckskin sack with a draw string slung to the left lapel of his coat. He did not take one of Fisher's vests after discarding the one he had been wearing, remarking that they were a nuisance and he was tired of wearing them.

After putting on the boy's shoes, Tracy took a seat in the corner, where he could watch two sides of the house from the windows, and set his rifle in the corner. He swung the revolver around where he could reach it handily and then told Mrs. Fisher to prepare him some sandwiches to take with him. She sliced up two loaves of bread and buttered the pieces well and then boiled a large piece of bacon to place between the layers. These sandwiches and some boiled eggs were afterward placed in a gunny sack from which Tracy removed the upper part, and slung across his back with a piece of bale rope. While waiting for the sandwiches to be prepared, Tracy chatted freely with Fisher and his son.

Tells of Killing Breece

"I shot and killed two men near Bothell yesterday," he said, *"and last night killed two men at Fremont. One of them I killed with my revolver and the other with my rifle. The man I killed with the revolver I shot twice."*

The story he had already told about killing Merrill, his companion, he repeated. He said Merrill had been the cause of his imprisonment, and he "never had any love for him anyway."

He exhibited his rifle, which he stroked lovingly, saying it had got him out of a good deal of trouble. He drew attention to the bead, or front sight, which had been filed down fine and smoked. He said the man who prepared it that way for him knew his business, because accurate, quick aim could be taken with it. He said that so far as aiming was concerned, that made little difference, except at a distance, because he shot from the hip without aim when close to a man.

"I have 160 cartridges here," he added, after praising his rifle and telling of his methods of shooting, "and before they get me I will have a good many less."

Takes His Departure

When Tracy was ready to leave, he said he guessed he would have to tie all the members of the family and leave them to be found by some of the neighbors. He asserted that he would not like to tie Mrs. Fisher and the little girls, but the exigencies of the situation demanded it. Just then, Mrs. Fisher's baby girl, aged 18 months, toddled away from one of her sisters and tried to crawl up in her mother's lap. Tracy surveyed the little one intently for a minute, as if in deep thought, then remarked:

"No, I will not tie you people up, because somebody will have to attend to that baby, and if I left its mother loose to look after it, she could release the others. But one thing I want you to do, and that is to give me a solemn promise that you will not tell anybody I have been here for the next forty-eight hours."

He made Fisher give the promise and afterward his son. Then he asked that the wife and girls, who understood English imperfectly, be notified. He cautioned Fisher against leaving the house or permitting any of his family to do so for some time after he had gone. He then took Fisher's name and informed him that he had

no money but would remember him, and if he succeeded in making his escape would some day reward him
for giving him the clothing and food.

"I'm not trying to hurt anybody except those that are
after me," he said as he walked away from the house.
"I'm not going to forget the people that have shown me
favors."

Climbs Back Fence

When he left the house, Tracy climbed the back fence
and walked northwest past Charley and George Baker's
house, about three hundred yards away, and in the
direction of another road, the location of which had
been explained to him at his request by Fisher. From
the window, he could be seen to glance back several
times until he reached the edge of the woods, through a
short stretch of which he had to go to reach the road.

All day Friday, Fisher and his family remained at
home, not daring to go outside of their yard. Yesterday
morning a friend named Taylor happened to pass
Fisher's house and walked in to spend a few minutes.
He was told of Tracy's visit and cautioned by Fisher not
to mention it to anybody, as the convict had threatened
to return and kill the whole family if anything was said
of his appearance. Taylor, however, telephoned briefly
what he had learned to Under-sheriff Corcoran. Deputy
Sheriff Oscar H. Springer, who speaks German fluent-
ly, was sent to the house of Fisher. He was accompanied
by Sheriff Zimmerman, of Snohomish County. Fisher
was not at home, having come to Seattle on business,
but the facts were learned from Mrs. Fisher. The clothing which the convict had discarded was brought to
town by Sheriff Zimmerman, but Deputy Springer
came in only as far as University station, where he
received telephonic orders to go back to Maple Leaf and
Pontiac and see if any boats were missing. The clothing
brought in by Zimmerman was readily identified by
Mrs. Van Horn as having been taken from her house by
Tracy.

Before Sheriff Zimmerman and Deputy Springer left

the house, they took one of the circulars of reward sent out for the two convicts, Merrill and Tracy, and folded the names under, after which the photographs were shown to each member of the family separately. All readily picked Tracy out as the man who had been at their house. This was true even in the case of the 5-year-old daughter.

Accompanied by a staff correspondent of the *Post-Intelligencer*, Deputy Spring again visited the Fisher ranch on his way back from University station to Maple Leaf and Pontiac. The facts of Tracy's appearance at the house were there a second time related to Springer in German by Mrs. Fisher, and by him given to the correspondent.

"I would have poisoned Tracy," emphatically declared Mrs. Fisher, "but he watched me too closely. I had the poison in the house, but could not get a chance to put it in the sandwiches. I would have been afraid to put it in the food he ate here, because he might have killed us all when it began to work on his system, but if I had got a chance I would have put it in the sandwiches, and then he would have died after taking it before he could have got back to the house.

"Once I went to the cupboard where the poison is in a bottle on the top shelf, but he kept his eyes on me, and I had to get a cup and saucer instead."

Meanwhile, Frank Scott, the crew member aboard the launch *N. & S.* who had persuaded Tracy to tell him the location of Merrill's body so that he could find it and claim the state of Oregon reward he thought to be $6,000, told a reporter he had changed his mind about quitting his oyster-picking job and living in the lap of luxury at taxpayer expense. He gave two reasons for his decision: first, that the reward seemed to have been reduced to $1,500; second, that he might not get it even if he did locate the remains.

"I shall return to work on the oyster lands Monday," he said mournfully. "There seems to be a disposition not to pay the reward for the recovery of Merrill's body, so I don't intend to go to any unnecessary trouble in the matter."

For a different reason, Mrs. Van Horn, the plucky woman

whose silent nod to the grocery boy while under Tracy's gun had brought Sheriff Cudihee and his posse to her home near Bothell and precipitated the shootout that had killed three men, also made an announcement to the press:

> *Mrs. Van Horn firmly refused to sit for her picture, saying she had a surfeit of notoriety already. She sat in the sheriff's private office talking to a few, while prying eyes in the front room strained for a glimpse of the woman who has become so suddenly famous. She is plainly a nervy woman, but her experiences with hold-ups have made her uneasy. She asked that a guard be placed on her house until Tracy is disposed of, as she fears that he may get hold of a paper and find out how much she has told about him. In that case, if he should happen to double back past her house, she thinks he would stop and take a shot at her.*

Though admitting that Sheriff Cudihee and his possemen were running down every Tracy-sighting reported to them, a news writer labeled one incident "a howling farce." While cruising down Sammamish Slough toward Lake Washington, crewmen aboard the steamer *Acme* saw a man answering Tracy's description walking across a field near Blythe's Bridge, a mile from Bothell. Both the officers and the passengers aboard the boat thought the man was "moving stealthily," which immediately drew their suspicion.

When the man noticed the steamer and the people aboard it pointing accusingly at him, he became even "stealthier", shifting the gunny sack and the buckskin bag he was carrying from one shoulder to another and changing his grip on what appeared to be a .30-.30 caliber Winchester rifle from one hand to the other, as if getting ready to use it. Despite the danger of the situation, five brave officers and passengers prepared to risk their lives after the boat docked by arming themselves with revolvers, rifles, and shotguns and following the stealthy suspect as he entered a barn next door to a farmhouse. A *P-I* reporter described the ensuing action.

"The mysterious individual turned out to be a farmer carrying a young pig home in the sack. He had his gun along as a matter of protection."

Which he almost needed . . .

Next day, another woman claiming to be Tracy's wife showed up in Tacoma, a newspaper there reported.

> *She goes by the name of Ely, and lives in an alley at the rear of Tacoma Avenue. She has been following the newspaper accounts of the convict's 27 days of flight, but declares she has no further interest in him.*

When she read the report that Merrill had secretly given the police information which resulted in Tracy's arrest and conviction three years ago, she said she knew Tracy would settle with Merrill if the opportunity offered itself. When shown the statement of Mrs. Van Horn that Tracy had told her he had read a newspaper account of Merrill's duplicity, the former Mrs. Tracy said:

"You may put it down for the truth that Tracy killed Merrill, just as he said he did."

Because human trackers were having no luck picking up Tracy's trail, the Seattle authorities decided to try bloodhounds again, asking the Washington State Prison in Walla Walla to put the handler and his best dogs aboard a train scheduled to leave Walla Walla at 9 p.m. that night and be set out on the Auburn siding between Seattle and Tacoma by 6 a.m. the following morning.

Pending the arrival of the trackers, the editor of the *Oregonian* assigned the task of writing a definitive article on the use of bloodhounds to one of his best writers. But before it could be published, Harry Tracy did the unexpected again—hijacking a boat and crossing Puget Sound to the Olympic Peninsula.

Newspaper clipping
Sheriff Edward Cudihee

Newspaper clipping
Guard E.M. Carson, of Walla Walla, and his bloodhounds.

Chapter Seven

Flight of Fancy

TRACY'S HOT TRAIL

Holds Up Family
on Bainbridge Island.
GETS CLOTHES AND PROVISIONS

Binds and Gags Four, Impresses a
Boatman and Embarks on Puget
Sound—Now Said to Be in
Vicinity of Whatcom.

By taking the longest jump he had yet made in his month-long flight, Harry Tracy escaped the net spread for him in the Bothell area. Confronting a Japanese fisherman at Meadow Point, where he had first landed from the gasoline launch a week ago, he forced the frightened young man to take him across the twelve miles of Puget Sound's often rough inland waters to Port Madison on Bainbridge Island. There, he dismissed the youth, warning him that he would be killed by Tracy's pals if he ever told anybody about the trip.

"The Japanese is still keeping quiet," a reporter wrote later, without revealing how *he* found out about what must have been a terrifying trip.

As a member of a small group of recent immigrants from Japan, it is unlikely that the young fisherman spoke English well enough to give the reporter much of an interview, even if he had been inclined to do so. At that place and time, the Pacific Northwest was becoming the new home for two classes of people: "Emigrants" and "Immigrants," the distinction being that most of the former were native-born Americans emigrating from the East to the West, while the latter were immigrating from Europe or the Orient. In time to come, most of them would learn to speak English and become good American citizens, but for many of them the melting-pot process was just beginning.

Landing near the home of a stump-rancher named John Johnson, Tracy watched the house for an hour to see how many people were there. Finding only two men, a woman, and two children in the house, he entered it, announcing that he had intended to kill everyone there and take over the place for a few days, then adding:

"But after seeing your pretty little girl, I will kill no one if you will mind me. I will be here all day."

Later, John Johnson, who was operating a logging operation and a small farm near Port Madison, and his wife took a steamer to Seattle and spent several hours at the police station telling their story to the authorities and the press. Because Johnson himself was a recent immigrant from Sweden with a poor command of English, while his wife was an Englishwoman and better able to express herself, she did most of the talking.

It was about two o'clock Saturday afternoon and she was at work in the kitchen, she said, when she heard a knock on the rear door of the house. When she opened it, she saw John Anderson, their hired man, standing there with a stranger. When she asked them what they wanted, the stranger said:

"I hate to trouble you, ma'am, but I'm being followed by a lot of men around this part of the country and I'm very hungry. I'd like something to eat as soon as you can fix it for me."

"My God!" she gasped, recognizing him from pictures she had seen in the newspapers. "You're Tracy!"

"Yes, I'm Tracy," he answered politely. "But you have nothing to fear. All I want is something to eat. If I get it and you make no fuss, you will not be harmed."

So frightened that she ran screaming from the house, she was caught and restrained by the hired man, John Anderson, who, as Tracy came outside and raised his rifle, cried:

"Don't run or he'll shoot you! Do what he tells you!"

Still breathless and trembling, she quieted down. Tracy scolded her.

"That was a foolish thing to do. If you had kept on running, I would have shot you."

"You frightened me to death."

"There is no need for you to be scared. I told you that if you acted sensibly you would not be hurt and I meant it. Now come into the house and get me something to eat."

The three of them went into the house and she began cooking a meal. Her husband was working in a hayfield and did not come to the house for an hour and a half, Mrs. Johnson told the authorities. Her ten-year-old son, Phillip, was in the kitchen, but Tracy paid little attention to him, apparently feeling that the youngster could do him no harm.

When she put bread and cheese on the table, Tracy said what he really wanted was fresh red meat. She said there was none in the house. Did she have any eggs? Yes, she had plenty of them. Then fry me some, he ordered, with bacon or ham if you have it. Finding some ham, she fried it and four eggs, which she served with bread, cheese, and coffee.

"All the time he was eating," she said, "he carried his rifle across his knees and had his revolver laid on the table at the right side of his cup of coffee, where he could get his hand on it quickly. He appeared very much afraid of dogs. Once when one barked while he was eating, he half rose to his feet and grasped his revolver. He asked whose dog it was, and when I told him I guessed it was owned by somebody living in the neighborhood, he sat down again and resumed his meal."

When he had finished eating, he asked Mrs. Johnson if she had any recent newspapers. Finding three copies of the *Post-Intelligencer*, she gave them to him. Leaning back in his chair, he perused them intently, now and then commenting on something that caught his attention. He was particularly interested in the account of his visit to the Van Horn home.

"Mrs. Van Horn was a mighty brave little woman," he said approvingly.

"Yes," Mrs. Johnson agreed. "But when the grocery boy came around, she told him you were there."

"No, she didn't," Tracy said. "She simply nodded her head in my direction. But that was enough. Which only proves her nerve. I have a whole lot of respect for that woman."

Growing bolder as time passed, Mrs. Johnson asked Tracy if he had really killed Merrill, as some newspapers were reporting. Yes, he answered, he'd killed his former partner. Why? she asked. Because he was a coward and tended to hold them back in their flight. Also because Merrill had been responsible for getting Tracy arrested and put in prison in the first place.

"So I killed him and hid the body in the brush."

"Where?"

That was none of her business, Tracy snapped.

"He said the killing at Fremont was a pretty bad affair," Mrs. Johnson told the authorities. "He explained that all he wanted to do was get away, and if they had let him alone he would have left without hurting anybody. If he were the bloodthirsty villain he was being made out to be, he said, he could have killed twenty more men than he had, for many times while hiding in the brush he had had bunches of unsuspecting possemen in his gunsights and slipped away without pulling the trigger."

At about this time, Mrs. Johnson's husband came in from the fields, saw the strange man in the house, and asked her who he was. Earlier, she had told Tracy that her husband was Swedish and did not speak English very well, causing Tracy to warn her:

"Don't try any foreign language on me. I want to know what you're saying. When your husband comes in, tell him to speak English."

After she did so, Tracy repeated his promise not to harm them if they did as they were told. He asked what time it was, Johnson answering half past three. Tracy said he wanted some clothing before he left.

"He took my husband and Anderson into one of the bedrooms, where there were two beds, selected a suit belonging to Anderson, and put it on. He cautioned Phillip and me not to leave the house or he would kill us."

Shutting the door while he changed clothes, Tracy made the two men go to a far corner of the room, laying his revolver on the bed and keeping a close eye on them. The suit he took was a new one, Johnson said, with a black coat and vest, and black pants with a fine gray stripe. He also took a pair of Johnson's black shoes and his sou'wester hat, along with some under-clothing and an extra pair of pants. Finding a brown crusher hat hanging on the wall, he took that, too.

Mrs. Johnson said after Tracy changed clothes, he opened the door so that she could see what he was doing. He took a pair of red blankets off one bed and a pair of blue ones off the other, remarking as he did so that his thing of lying around in the woods at night with no bedding wasn't what it was cracked up to be.

"He took my husband's watch and solid gold chain," Mrs. Johnson said, "Anderson's silver watch and gold chain, a gold-filled watch that belonged to a man who died in Seattle, and a ladies' solid gold watch that I was keeping for the son of the same man. This made three men's watches and a ladies' watch he took, all having gold chains. He also took my husband's sil-ver match box and two gold rings."

Placing the blankets, watches, and the clothes he was wear-ing when he came to the Johnson home in a good-sized valise belonging to his involuntary host, Tracy came into the kitchen and asked Mrs. Johnson to give him some provisions to take with him: twenty-five pounds of flour, a large-sized piece of ham, half a pound of coffee, half a pound of sugar, a little salt, a small frying pan, a small lard pail, and some matches. These were all placed in a gunny sack, making a sizable load to be car-ried. But he had planned for that, too, as would soon be learned.

"When time came for the evening meal," Mrs. Johnson said, "I spread the table in the dining room and started to get him something to eat. He reminded me that there were others to be fed, and that we all should all sit at the same table. My hus-band said he had to go milk the cow. Tracy told him to go ahead, but that if he gave the alarm he would kill me and Phillip."

When her husband returned from milking the cow, they all sat down at the table and began to eat, Tracy with his rifle rest-ing between his knees and his revolver lying on the table beside his plate, the two men sitting on the other side of the table where he could see them but be out of their reach.

"I cooked eggs and potatoes," she said, "fried some ham, warmed up some brown beans and stew I'd done earlier, and brought out some preserves. Tracy ate a good meal, though not nearly as big a one as he'd eaten earlier. The rest of us ate fairly well because we saw that he would not harm us if we did nothing to excite his anger or suspicion."

After the meal, he asked Johnson a lot of questions about the Hood Canal region and settlements in the area where he might get something to eat. Several times he asked what time it was, saying he'd be leaving when it got dark, which at that this of year would be around nine o'clock.

"He said he would have to bind and gag us, though he did not like to do that to a woman or a pretty little girl," Mrs. Johnson said. "The rope he used he took from the clothesline, having Anderson go out to cut it while he watched him with his rifle."

Forcing Anderson to help him bind and gag all the members of the family, though cautioning the hired man not to tie up the little girl or Mrs. Johnson too tightly, Tracy then bound Anderson, too, for he said he wanted to take a basin of hot water off the kitchen stove and shave before he set out on the next leg of his trip.

"When he was ready to leave the house, he released Anderson and told him to come along," Mrs. Johnson said. "I could hear him but could not see him at this time. I heard him tell Anderson that when they got to the boat he was going to bind him to the seat and tie his hands to the oars, so he would be powerless to offer resistance."

A muscular, husky young man used to hard physical labor, Anderson would have the power to carry the full valise and gunny sacks filled with food supplies down to the fourteen-foot-long, relatively new, white-painted rowboat lying at the dock below the house, then pick up the oars and row Tracy wherever he wanted to go.

"I lay quiet for an hour after he was gone," Mrs. Johnson said. "He did not tie me too tightly, saying he did not care to hurt me with the rope, so I easily released myself. Then I untied my husband, who ran to the house of Deputy Sheriff McKay and told him what had happened. "

In summing up her experiences with the murderous escaped convict, Mrs. Johnson showed herself to be as plucky a woman as Mrs. Van Horn, whom Tracy had praised for her nerve. Since nobody got hurt and the food Tracy had been fed and had stolen were minor matters, the only items she really missed were the new blankets, the gold watches, and her husband's shoes, which were expensive to replace.

"The provisions and blankets and clothing we can spare, I guess," she said philosophically. "However, our hired man, John Anderson, will miss his suit of new clothing, which had just been finished for him by the tailor."

So far as Anderson was concerned, his chances for ever wearing his new suit looked rather dim at the moment. Ordering him to pick up the oars and start rowing, Tracy set a course southeast down Puget Sound in the direction of Olympia, then changed his mind and turned northeast toward Whidbey Island and points unknown.

After Mrs. Johnson freed herself and her husband notified Deputy Sheriff McKay, who lived at Port Madison, of what had happened, McKay secured a boat and crossed to Seattle, which he reached at three o'clock in the morning. By the time word was sent to Sheriff Cudihee in Bothell and he charted the tug *Sea Lion*, on which he set out in pursuit of Tracy, the convict not only had a fifteen-hour head-start, but no one knew where he was or was going.

"The supposition is that after forcing the scared farm hand to row all night," a reporter wrote gloomily, "Tracy will kill Anderson, sink the boat, and disappear in the wild forests of Northwestern Washington, where he can live many days on his supply of food and then reappear to attempt another long jump toward liberty."

As usually happened when predictions were made regarding Harry Tracy's future behavior, this one was wrong on all counts except one . . .

No less an expert than "Cub" Merrill, yet another brother of Tracy's former convict friend, David Merrill, declared that what

Tracy *really* was trying to do was reach his friends in Whatcom County, near Bellingham, in the extreme northern part of Washington state adjacent to British Columbia.

"While intoxicated Saturday night," a reporter wrote, "Cub Merrill said that the murderer was on his way to that place. Arrangements have been made to meet him there."

Another source said that Tracy had relatives near Bothell who had helped him escape the posse. "They state that the murderer's brother-in-law lives somewhere in the woods about fifteen miles north of the town, and that to reach him has been Tracy's chief object since he left Thurston County in the steam launch. The mysterious buggy seen on the county road near Wayne Friday night was driven, in the opinion of Bothell people, by the brother-in-law."

> *Tracy, the escaped Oregon convict, has completely slipped away from the Seattle officers. His whereabouts are a mystery, as are those of the man he made accompany him on starting out for a cruise about Puget Sound Saturday.*

For several days, the only news on the Tracy front was that the bloodhounds and their handler, Guard E.M. Carson, had arrived from the Walla Walla Penitentiary and were ready, willing, and able to follow the scent of the outlaw, if only they could be put upon it. Being aboard the tug *Sea Lion* as it chugged up and down Puget Sound under Sheriff Cudihee's direction, the only smell the sensitive nostrils of the dogs got was that of fresh, damp, salty sea air. While the chase was pending, the editor of the *Oregonian* judged this to be a good time to publish his expert's well-researched article entitled:

THE BLOODHOUND

> *The experiences of the Tracy and Merrill chase have not served to increase the reputation of the bloodhound as a man-finder. Again and again the dogs from Walla Walla were put upon the trail, only to pursue it with loud outcry for a little while and then lose it altogether. Wherever it crossed water or wet ground, it was certain*

to be lost; and in Western Oregon, where water or wet ground is encountered every few rods, the bloodhound is not likely ever to be a certain or a valuable resource. He may serve a good purpose in dry country like Eastern Oregon or Eastern Washington, but efforts to work with him here is likely to prove effort wasted.

A writer in the Century deals at length with the bloodhound in America, and corrects some general impressions concerning his character, among other things, the notion he is a brute of savage and ferocious instinct and habit. His eagerness in the chase, this writer declares, proceeds from no brutal or savage disposition, for when he overtakes his quarry he does not assault it, but fawns upon it in the greatest apparent delight. He is, in truth, a most amiable animal, so much so that breeders recommend him as a pet and companion for young children where docility and kindness are essential qualities.

The bad name of the bloodhound is due to his connection with the search for criminals, in which he is everywhere employed, and especially to his use in the South in times past in the business of hunting down runaway slaves. The old Southern "nigger dog" was a brute of great ferocity, but he was not rightly speaking a bloodhound. It was found that a cross of the bloodhound with the Great Dane and with some one of the very savage families of dogs produced a brute in which the trailing power was but slightly impaired, but with savage instinct and habit to which the genuine bloodhound is a stranger. This terrible creature was a great ally to the slave hunter because he inspired the negroes with terror, serving not merely to find those who had absconded, but to prevent others from following their example.

So great had become the popular hatred of the animal which in the South went by the name of "nigger dog" and in the North by bloodhound that when the Northern armies marched South, special orders were issued to kill every such dog that was found. The

greatest breeding pack of these dogs was on the planta-
tion of Jefferson Davis, in Mississippi, and it is hardly
necessary to say that the boys of Grant's army specially
detailed to search out and destroy bloodhounds took
especial delight in doing a thorough job when they
came to the Davis kennels. George S. Meeker, of
Beatrice, Neb., personally killed 47 dogs at the Davis
place.

It is believed that the bloodhound in the United
States was absolutely extinct at the close of the Civil
War; and he was not again noted until 1888, when the
breed made its reappearance at a New York bench show,
the three individuals then exhibited being imported
dogs brought over by the principal breeder of such dogs
in England. With these three animals a breeding estab-
lishment was set up in Vermont and since that time oth-
ers have been established in Massachusetts, Kentucky,
and Nebraska. There is a great demand for the dogs
from prisons. All that can be produced find ready sales
at prices which make a well-bred bloodhound a much
better piece of property than the average horse.

Several packs of bloodhounds are kept in a constant
state of training in the Middle West, and employed by
their owners for hunting down criminals, the best
known being the art of a Dr. Fulton, who devotes him-
self exclusively to the business. His pack consists of 13
animals, all trained by himself and always employed
under his own immediate direction. They have become
celebrated all over the country and they are in frequent
employment. They have brought many a criminal to
justice and have never failed to run down their man
when placed on the trail within a reasonable period of
time. Of course, these dogs are kept in condition all the
time and in perfect training under one man whose word
they obey implicitly. Effective as they have proved them-
selves to be in unnumbered cases, it is doubtful that,
separated from their companions and in the hands of
strangers or men unaccustomed to the work, they would
be of much practical account.

It is doubtful if the bloodhound will ever be found very serviceable in a country like our own, broken by streams and abounding in patches of damp meadow. Possibly a highly trained pack like that of Dr. Fulton might do something, but the conditions are not such as to promote the creation of such a pack. It is only in centers like the Mississippi Valley, where there is a great deal of work in the line of criminal hunting, that there is employment enough to justify the maintenance of a pack of hounds in effective training. Good work may sometimes be done by isolated pairs of dogs like those lent to the Tracy and Merrill hunt by the Walla Walla Penitentiary, but as a rule—and especially in this wet country—they will be found to be practically useless.

Whether Harry Tracy read the article is not known. Though recently he had expressed his fear of dogs, earlier he had told the men who had rowed him across the Columbia River that bloodhounds did not worry him. On one occasion, he would prove that he knew exactly what to do to throw them temporarily off his trail.

While dozens of officers were looking for Tracy in half a dozen widely scattered places across, up, and down Puget Sound, he suddenly re-surfaced for the fourth time in what was becoming his favorite spot—Meadow Point, just north of Seattle. Landing from the boat borrowed from John Johnson in Port Madison, whose oars still were being pulled by the hired man John Anderson, Tracy struck a trail leading to the home of Charles Gerrells, one mile north of the town of Renton, at two o'clock Tuesday afternoon. After spending the rest of the day hiding out in a ravine, Tracy forced Anderson, whom he was treating like a veritable galley slave, to row him across an inlet to a point near Newell's Mill, where the boat was beached and abandoned. It was found and identified a short while later by Deputy Sheriff McKay, who passed the word along to Sheriff Cudihee and his deputies. The chase resumed.

Meanwhile at the Gerrells' home, what can only be described as a "romantic interlude" was taking place.

"The Tracy whom May Baker, an 18-year-old girl, will remember for the rest of her life," a reporter wrote, "is a gallant, tender-hearted man, with a prodigious love for little children, a conversationalist of brilliancy, a merry-hearted 'josher,' a man with a decided respect for womanhood, but, above all, a man with iron nerve."

Having spent more than four hours in the Gerrells' house with Mrs. Charles Gerrells, a neighbor lady named Mrs. W.J. Mckinney, several children, and Harry Tracy, Miss May Baker had a good opportunity to evaluate the convict's character, however misguided her starry-eyed appraisal may have been. Certainly the reporter's rhetoric sounds a trifle overblown as he writes:

> The story of Tracy's visit to the Gerrells' home reads like one of Alexander Dumas' romances. Nothing that Jesse James ever did in the way of daring and audacity could equal the calmness of the now famous outlaw while in the house. He treated the women with the greatest courtesy. He entertained them with his conversation, and soothed Mrs. McKinney's six-year-old child, Ada McKinney, when she became frightened.

Confined to the house with Tracy for most of the afternoon, the last hour of which they knew that the house was surrounded by heavily armed posse members who might choose to attack at any time, the involuntary captives later had nothing but praise for their treatment by the outlaw, who never showed the least apprehension. In fact, when Miss Baker complained about their being cooped up all day long:

> Tracy proposed that they should dance to while away the time. He carried water for the dinner, chopped wood and made himself generally useful, carried on a mild flirtation with Miss Baker, and for several hours engaged her in intellectual battle.

So many new facets of the fugitive's character were exposed, the ladies declared later, that they were unable to give any analysis of his overall personality. On one occasion when he looked out the window and saw a newspaper man walking down the railroad track not far away, he turned to Miss Baker and called:

"There goes the posse's advance agent!"

Intimating that he was fleeing more from reporters who wanted to interview him than from law officers, Tracy said he regarded newsmen as more dangerous than prison guards.

Tracy's first contact with the ladies had been made that morning, after the convict and his reluctant companion, John Anderson, had spent what was left of the night hiding out in a brushy ravine near the place on Puget Sound where they had left the boat. The Gerrells home was situated two miles up the track of the old Columbia & Puget Sound Railroad. When morning came, the two men moved inland, journeying slowly, stopping now and then to rest in the dense brush beside the road.

Miss Baker and Mrs. McKinney were out picking blackberries, that lovely mid-summer morning. From his place of concealment, Tracy watched them for some time without revealing his presence, until Charles Gerrells, an eighteen-year-old boy, came along. Stepping out into the open, Tracy said, "Hey, stop a moment."

The boy stopped and stared, as did the two women when they joined him.

"I guess you've heard of me," Tracy said, giving the ladies his most winning smile.

Not too sure of herself, Mrs. McKinney murmured, "You wouldn't be Tracy, would you?"

"Oh, no, he couldn't be!" Miss Baker gasped, doing her best to deny what she feared was true. "I don't know who you are."

"I *am* Tracy. But don't be afraid. I won't hurt you."

"Well, Mr. Tracy," Mrs. McKiney said as she recovered from the shock, "I am glad to see you."

"I would never have known you from your picture," Miss Baker exclaimed.

"Ah, now, you're jollying me," Tracy said with a disarming chuckle. "But don't be afraid. I've never harmed a woman in my life."

When he learned that the Gerrells' home was a short distance away, he told the party that they would all have to go there. Before they reached the house, he sent Charles Gerrells ahead to warn his mother that she was about to have company, adding:

"Tell her I'll bring harm to no one in her family."

When the group entered the house, Tracy took off his hat and sat down in the living room. Within five minutes, Miss Baker said later, he had quieted the fears of everyone except Mrs. Gerrells, who remained "somewhat nervous" throughout his prolonged stay in her home. As for May Baker herself, she studied him closely, noting that he looked fresh and strong. Except for his eyes, his face was serene and pleasant. She did find his eyes disturbing. They were an unnatural shade of dark blue, she said, and rolled about restlessly whenever he made a threat regarding what he would do to his attackers if cornered, as he did on several occasions.

He did not look unusually thin and appeared to be in fine physical condition, she said. Mentally, she thought he was "one of the keenest men I ever met." He was dressed in a black suit, and wore a black felt hat. His trousers were much too short, "a matter of much merriment to himself. He had no tie or collar, but had jewelry to spare."

When he first came into the house, Mrs. McKinney's six-year-old daughter, Ada, began to cry. Mrs. Gerrells looked terrified. Tracy called the child to him, saying soothingly, "Now, now, little girl, don't cry. I won't let anyone harm you."

Some hours later when tension grew inside the house as possemen were seen closing in outside, the little girl crept to Tracy's side for protection.

Whether eighteen-year-old Charles Gerrells was so awed by Tracy that the convict assumed the young man would do whatever he was told to do—or Tracy naively misjudged him— is not clear. But for some reason Tracy gave him two of the watches he had taken from the Johnson home, told him to sell them in town, then use the proceeds to buy a couple of revolvers.

"I want two .45 Colts with six-inch barrels," Tracy said, "and two boxes of cartridges. Now, if you 'peach' on me, kid, you will hear from me."

"I am kind of scared of you, Tracy," the boy admitted shyly, as he got ready to leave for town. "But I will help you."

"If he betrays me," Tracy told Mrs. Gerrells while her son was still close enough to hear the threat, "I will kill your two other children."

Feeling that he had made sure Charles Gerrells would do as he had been told, Tracy watched the young man leave the house, then turned to Mrs. Gerrells, who had burst into tears, and said soothingly:

"That was only a bluff. You have nothing to fear from me. I have a mother who is reading the papers to see if I am caught. I wouldn't care about this scrape I am in if it were not for her. God knows, lady, I wouldn't harm a hair on your head, let alone these innocent little children."

As he uttered these heartfelt words, Miss Baker told a reporter later, ". . . tears stood in his eyes and for the first time the bravado in his manner left him."

Whether the tears he had shed and the bravado he had lost were sincere, no one could later say. But if he had known that young Charles Gerrells was heading not for the pawn shop to sell the watches but was making a bee-line toward the sheriff's office carrying word to the authorities that Harry Tracy had taken over the Gerrells' home, the tears he was shedding might have been real.

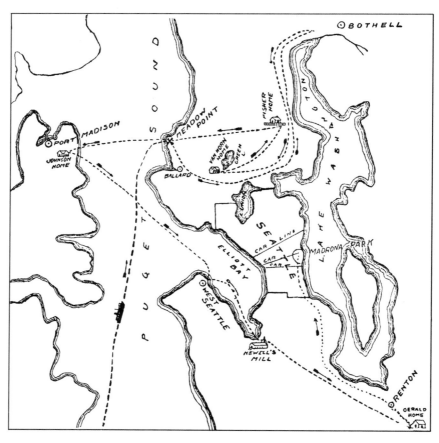

Harry Tracy's travels in the Puget Sound area.

CHAPTER EIGHT

ROMANTIC INTERLUDE

"**I**nformation conveyed by eighteen-year-old Charles Gerrells," a reporter wrote in the *P-I*, July 9, "indicated that Tracy now was a visitor at his father's home on the Columbia and Puget Sound Railroad, one mile from the town of Renton. The news was acted upon with vigor by the handful of deputies who chanced to be quartered in the Sheriff's office."

Since acting with vigor always seemed to require that a reporter be present to record the ensuing events, a newsman named C.B. Yandell, whose paper was not identified, joined a posse led by Deputy Sheriff McClellan, two policemen, and what soon became a rather large crowd of eager manhunters within a few minutes of receiving the information.

"They boarded a Renton railroad passenger car," a reporter wrote, "which had been promised for the exclusive use of the deputies from the downtown terminus. It was crowded, and, though an effort was made to prevail upon the conductor to obey the instructions which the management had presumably given him and clear the car, he declined to do so, and more than half an hour was lost on the run to Renton."

At some point, the deputies and newsman Yandell switched to a caboose, which was quickly attached to an engine, and the party started up the track toward the Gerrells' home without further loss of time. The engine was run under the sheriff's instructions to a point one-half mile north of the Gerrells' house, where the train slowed down enough to let two deputies drop off. The engineer then drove the train back toward Renton, again slowing down within three hundred yards of the house to let Deputy McClellan and reporter Yandell leave the caboose and conceal themselves in the brush.

Crawling carefully forward through the thick undergrowth, the two men reached a spot 150 yards away from where Harry Tracy sat chatting with the three ladies of the house. The two deputies who had left the train farther up the track moved down the west side of the river into positions where Tracy would be pinned between them and the main body of the sheriff's posse when it showed up, as it was expected to do any minute now.

The minute proved to be a long one. Though the four men had taken up their positions at 3:30 in the afternoon, Deputy Sheriff Cook did not appear until 4:45; when he did, only a fraction of the posse was with him. But eventually, Sheriff Cudihee, Guard Carson, and two leashed bloodhounds arrived. The moment for decisive action seemed near.

Meanwhile, Harry Tracy, Miss May Baker, and the two other ladies were spending a reasonably sociable afternoon together. After Miss Baker observed Tracy shedding tears at the thought of his mother, she sought to ease his pain by changing the subject, asking him:

"Mr. Tracy, why do you wear a mustache?"

"Oh, I don't know," he responded. "Why do you ask?"

"Because I don't like to see a man with a mustache," Miss Baker said archly.

"Have you got a razor around here?" rejoined Tracy, quick as a flash (so Miss Baker told a reporter later). "I'll shave it off."

From that moment until his departure, the reporter wrote, "the murderer and the three women were engaged in repartee."

Courteous as Tracy was to the ladies in the house, his treatment of the hired man he had abducted at Port Madison and forced to carry burdens, row the boat, and do whatever Tracy wanted him to do, was cruel and brutal. With his hands bound behind him and his ankles hobbled so that he could take only small steps, Anderson had been brought into the kitchen and made to sit on a stool without moving or speaking for the past two hours. Putting his rifle down in a corner of the living room, where he had been carrying on his repartee with the ladies, Tracy asked them to excuse him while he went into the kitchen, poured a basin of water at the sink, and washed himself. After a good scrubbing, he noticed Anderson sitting immobile and silent, jerked him to his feet, led him to the back porch, and pushed him down on a straight-backed wooden chair, grunting: "Sit there until I tell you to move."

When Mrs. Gerrells came into the kitchen and began preparing the evening meal, Tracy made himself useful by going out in the back yard to cut kindling and carry water from the spring. On one of his trips, the special train from Renton bearing possemen rumbled by, forcing Tracy to duck into the bushes to avoid being seen. When he went back into the house, he told Miss Baker what he had observed.

"They had a red-headed reporter aboard when they went up the track. I can always spot the newspaper men. When I am running from the posse, there is always a reporter about a mile in advance of the rest, with a camera in one hand and a big bunch of note paper in the other. But I dodge interviews. I can't waste my time."

"Oh, Mr. Tracy!" Miss Baker giggled. "You're so funny!"

Gazing at her thougtfully, he smiled and said, "I like you, Miss Baker. Where do you live?"

"I won't tell you!" she flared indignantly. Then, as curiosity got the better of her, she asked, "Why do you want to know?"

"Oh, I may go to town tonight and rob a jewlery store for you," he teased. "Is there anything you would especially like to have?"

He then joked Miss Baker about a ring she had on her left hand, a reporter wrote; she retorted with repartee in kind, "and the fun was fast and furious when they all sat down to dinner." Tracy went to the rear porch and led Anderson in. The two men sat on one side of the table and the women on the other. The children sat at the ends. Though Tracy ate very little, he was assiduous in his attention to the women and children.

"This is just like home," he declared. "You don't know how much I am enjoying your society."

"You spoiled our berry-picking expedition," Miss Baker complained.

"Well," Tracy said, "we'll all go berry-picking in a little while, if you like. I'll help you."

"But we'll be late getting back home to Seattle," Mrs. McKinney objected.

"That's all right," Tracy said gallantly. "I will steal the best buggy in the whole neighborhood and drive you home."

After much good natured chaff between Tracy, Miss Baker, and Mrs. McKinney, Tracy picked up an old newspaper and read about the Underwood case, a particularly brutal recent murder of a child by a man of that name.

"Now, there is a man who, in my opinion, is one of the biggest cowards in the state," Tracy said. "To go and kill an innocent baby! Why, hanging is too good for Underwood. He should be shown no mercy. Some of the papers say that I am a coward, but they don't know me. I kill men. I've never harmed a woman or a child in my whole life."

"But, Tracy," Miss Baker protested. "You shot Merrill in the back."

"That is an unjust charge," Tracy exclaimed. "The papers have the wrong story. When the newspaper men come around to interview you about my visit, tell them for me that I killed Merrill without treachery. He was a mean-spirited sort of man. When we quarreled and decided to fight, I was willing to be square. I always fight square. But I knew him. As we walked away ten paces from each other I watched him over my shoulder. At the eighth step, he turned to fire. I jumped around and let him have it. As he reeled and fell, I shot him again in the back. Then I walked up to his prostrate body and shot him in the head."

"But you needn't have killed Breece."

"I had to," Tracy said. "The newspapers have got the wrong story about that fight. I told Breece to fling down his gun. In a second we were locked in each other's arms. We struggled for barely a moment, when I raised my revolver and shot him. The men with us then started to run."

All the time this repartee was going on, the house was being surrounded by possemen. Tracy seemed unconcerned. His rifle was still leaning against the wall in a corner of the room, though his revolver was near at hand in the waistband of his trousers.

"We can wait here until dark," he said, getting up from the table, going to the window, and peering outside. "Then we'll walk down the track together. I'll go with you as far as Renton." Turning back into the room, he smiled at Miss Baker. "It will be a nice, moonlight walk, in very pleasant company."

"Well, I don't know about that," Miss Baker snapped peevishly. "It won't be very pleasant if deputies are shooting at us."

"But *I'll* be safe," Tracy joked. "You ladies will have to form a cordon around me. You'd do that for me, wouldn't you?"

"Oh, sure," Miss Baker said sarcastically. "We would like to get killed for you—I don't think."

Growing tired of bantering with Miss Baker, Tracy turned his attention to Mrs. Gerrells, first praising the quality of her cooking, then complaining about his own crude efforts at baking bread. After hearing a number of his questions about the proper way to bake bread, Mrs. McKinney asked rather testily:

"Why don't you take your wife in Portland along with you on your travels? She could do the cooking."

Tracy shook his head. "The woman in Portland that the police are watching is not my wife. She is Dave Merrill's sister. Her family was not treating her right, so I took pity on her, sending her money when she got sick and trying to take care of her." He turned his attention back to Mrs. Gerrells. "By the way, I liked the Graham bread we had at dinner. I wish I knew how to make it."

"Oh, dear," Miss Baker said, trying retrieve his attention, "I feel tired of staying in the house all day, doing nothing. Can't we go out?"

"Do you dance?" Tracy asked.

"Why, yes, I like to dance."

"Does anyone here play the piano?"

"Why do you ask?" Mrs. McKinney said.

"Well, I thought if one of you ladies could play the piano, Miss Baker and I would dance to while away the time."

"But there's no piano," Mrs. Gerrells said.

"In that case, we have a problem."

By now, law officers, possemen, and reporters completely surrounded the house. When a burly, mustached man wearing a deputy's badge walked across the yard and knocked on the front door, Tracy picked up his rifle, herded Miss Baker and Mrs. McKinney into the kitchen, half closed the door, then motioned for Mrs. Gerrells to deal with the posseman. Recognizing the man as a butcher from Renton, she asked him what he wanted.

"Is Tracy here?" he demanded.

"Why would you think that?" she stalled, well aware of the fact that the convict's rifle was aimed at her and the intruder.

Refusing to answer her question, the man entered the house, crossed the living room, then paused just outside the partially closed kitchen door, which was blocked by Miss Baker, who was being covered by Tracy's revolver.

"Is Tracy in there?" the possemnan asked belligerently.

"What would Tracy be doing in the kitchen?" Miss Baker answered scornfully, doing her best to look as if that were a stupid question.

Baffled by her reply, the shame-faced posseman muttered an apology, turned, and left the house.

When Miss Baker told Tracy she had smelled whiskey on the posseman's breath, he first complimented her on her behavior, then made some comments on the evils of alcohol.

"Liquor is a dangerous thing and should be avoided," he said. "I am glad to say I have never been drunk. A man like myself dare not touch the stuff. It dulls the brain and is a curse to humanity." Wanting to make the conversation more general, he abruptly changed the the subject, asking Mrs. McKinney, "What nationality are you?"

"Scotch-Irish—and proud of it."

"Why, so am I!" Tracy exclaimed. He turned to Miss Baker. "And you?"

"I'm of English descent," Miss Baker said loftily. "I was born in Texas."

"I knew you were a Southern girl," Tracy said in admiration. "I knew it from your speech and because you are so plucky."

At six o'clock in the evening of the gray, rainy day, Tracy knew he should leave the house, but was reluctant to do so.

Looking ruefully down at his trousers, which reached only to his ankles, he said, "I wish my trousers were not so short. I think I'll go out and hold up one of the deputies and trade pants with him. Do you ladies see anybody along the railroad track whose trousers would fit me?"

Getting no response to his question, Tracy made another complaint. "You have beastly weather on Puget Sound. Why, it's rained all the time since I landed here. I think this is an unhealthy country."

Reading another meaning into that statement, one of the boys in the room snickered.

"No, I mean unhealthy in its ordinary sense," Tracy said. "Not just unhealthy for me."

"Well, of course that's what you mean," Miss Baker sniffed. "We all understood that."

Gazing out into the twilight, Tracy said reflectively, "I think I'll go in to Seattle tonight. Maybe to Clancy's place. Do you know where it is?"

"Of course not!" Mrs. McKinney said indignantly.

"Decent ladies *never* go there!" Miss Baker exclaimed, then added. "But I've heard—just *heard*, mind you—it's down near the water front."

"My apologies, ladies," Tracy said politely. "I know you'd *never* go near that kind of a place." Seeing the growing crowd of men outside as they moved along the railroad grade seeking better positions from which to watch the house, his face grew somber. "Look at them! They don't want to catch me so I can be punished. They're all after the reward money."

"A Seattle banker has just added one thousand dollars to the reward, I hear," Mrs. McKinney said.

"Do you know his name?"

"No, I don't."

"I'll find out," Tracy said grimly. "If he'll meet me face to face, I'll let him try to earn it."

Deciding to make his break now, Tracy slipped out the back door and made a cautious scout, checking possible lines of escape, returning in five minutes or so to announce his plans.

"Looks like they're not covering the river very well. I can't take Anderson with me, so I'll tie him up and leave him in the chicken house out back." Hearing Anderson groan in dismay, Tracy laughed harshly. "Don't complain, you dumb Swede. I've tied you up and left you in lots worse places. At least here you'll have a roof over your head and some chickens to keep you company."

Stripping two leather straps off a suitcase, Tracy used them to bind Anderson more firmly, gagged him, then started to take him out the back door, pausing to say:

"Goodbye, ladies. It was just like home."

Then he vanished into the gloom.

Later, the several dozen possemen who had been surrounding the house for the past two hours told varying stories of what they had seen or thought they had seen of Tracy as he attempted to slip through the screen they had thought they had placed around him. Moving down the slope behind the house to the west bank of the river, he crossed a field filled with chest-high weeds, carrying his rifle at the ready, seeing several possemen watching him from the railroad right-of-way above, ready to return their fire when they started shooting at him.

But they did not open fire, for two of them, at least, were newsmen armed with nothing more lethal than than cameras and pencils. Both of them thought he was a posseman—and a rather stupid one, at that—for one reporter called to another:

"There is a fool of a deputy exposing himself!"

Since the possemen would not fire at him, Tracy decided he would not shoot at them. A moment later, he vanished into the forest . . .

The same issue of the *Post-Intelligencer* that contained the story of Tracy's visit to the Gerrells' home published two other items of interest to readers of the continuing saga. The first was a three-column by five-inch photograph of a crowd of several hundred businessmen wearing dark suits and straw, derby, or rancher style hats as they milled around in front of a billboard erected before the *Post-Intelligencer* building in downtown Seattle, reading the latest news-flashes on the escaped convict's doings.

The other was a human-interest story elaborating on the background and character of the Indian manhunter mentioned briefly a week earlier, who had been pursuing Tracy ever since the chase began:

ON TRACY'S TRAIL

Jake Williams, of Cathlamet Reservation, Again in the Pursuit of the Murderer

The most picturesque character in the chase after Convict Tracy is Jake Williams, a native policeman of the Cathlamet Indian Reservation in Oregon. He joined Sheriff Cudihee yesterday, going with him to Port Madison. Williams followed hot on Tracy and Merrill's trail from the time they escaped from the penitentiary until they entered Thurston County. During the chase in the southern part of the state, he proved himself a regular human bloodhound. From the way he hunts his quarry, he will make life uneasy for the convict if he again gets in the vicinity of Tracy.

"I am only one Indian," he said yesterday, when asked why he pursued Tracy so relentlessly. "If I am killed, there are lots of other Indians in America. Tracy has killed innocent white men. If I had one hundred dollars, I would gladly give it just to get within one hundred feet of him."

Williams was born in Oregon City and is well educated. He went to the reservation six years ago and has been a policeman for the past two years. When the bloodhounds were sent after Tracy and Merrill in southern Washington, Williams followed close after the animals, being in advance of other pursuers. He is a typical Indian and steals silently through the forest when on the chase.

It is said by his Oregon friends that he rivals Tracy himself in endurance.

Soon after Tracy disappeared, the posse closed in on the Gerrells' house, with the newspaper reporters attempting to interview the ladies being put off by Mrs. Gerrells, who insisted that the much-abused John Anderson, whom Tracy had bound and gagged and left in the chicken coop, be turned loose. A reporter wrote:

> *Mrs. Gerrells stepped to the rear of the premises and called to Anderson, who up to this moment had lain bound in the chicken coop. He answered feebly. The thongs which bound him were quickly severed, and he tottered into the group of deputies, trembling and unable to speak.*

Regaining his faculties after being refreshed with stimulants and attention, John Anderson gave the officers information which established beyond a doubt that four men, whom he could not identify, were lending Harry Tracy every assistance within their power in his efforts to evade capture.

Tracy had first met the men on the raiload bridge near Renton, Anderson said, consulting with them briefly, addressing one of them as "Fred." On two occasions, Tracy had left Anderson bound and gagged while he disappeared with his four mysterious friends—for what purpose, Anderson could not say. Later, John Anderson would be encouraged to relate more details of his experiences. But right now covering the chase took precedence for the reporters.

Soon after Tracy slipped through the ranks of the posse, the bloodhounds were brought to the scene and given the scent by a piece of clothing the fugitive had left behind. Hot on the trail of the dogs was a reporter, who wrote:

> *Both dogs struck the trail leading down the stream, following it for a quarter of a mile and crossing the railroad track, only to double back and swim the river. It was afterward learned that two newspaper men saw Tracy cross the track at this point five minutes ahead of the dogs. He evidently forded the river a few minutes afterward, for hardly had the posse been re-distributed than both dogs picked up the trail on the west side of the river, and giving tongue in a manner which left no*

doubt but that they were close on their quarry trailed
almost due west.

Just when it seemed that the much-pursued outlaw had gone to ground because of the relentless pursuit of the reporters and the bloodhounds, Harry Tracy demonstrated why he had once boasted that bloodhounds did not worry him.

"Half way between Cedar River and Burrough's boathouse," a reporter wrote, "both dogs ran into cayenne pepper sprinkled on the outlaw's retreating footsteps. Their nostrils were filled with the fiery substance, and fully ten minutes were lost in relieving the dogs so that they could again exercise their sense of smell."

Not discouraged by this treacherous assault upon their olfactory organs, the dogs recovered and once more took to the trail, their deep, baying voices clearly declaring that they refused to be blocked by the wily tricks of man. Pressed to desperation, Tracy made a circle, re-crossing his trail, headed due north downhill, then plunged into the knee-deep, muddy shallows of Lake Washington. There then occurred a scene worthy of being immortalized on film, if only the technique, the equipment, and the crew had been available.

In an effort to throw the bloodhounds off his trail, Tracy climbed the trestlework of a streetcar track bridge that spanned a quarter-mile arm of the lake, got aboard a streetcar, rode it cross the lake, then got off and took to the water again. Tracking him to the base of the fifty-foot high trestle, the dogs tried to climb it, could not, and were taken by their handler, Guard Carson, to a spot where they could follow the scent across the trestle. When they had trouble with their legs slipping between the ties, Guard Carson took them to a nearby streetcar stop, hailed the next trolley car going the same way Tracy had gone, and got aboard.

Presumably, the thoroughly wet dogs were on a leash and Guard Carson was not charged a fare by the startled motorman, though whether the also wet deputies and newspaper reporters were asked to deposit tokens was not recorded. It seems reasonable to assume that at that hour of the evening swains and sweethearts dressed in party clothes heading into

Seattle for a night on the town would have been aboard the trolley, and that the bloodhounds, being wet, would shake themselves as dogs will do, with accompanying cries of anger from the swains and shrieks of dismay from the ladies. Unfortunately, no camcorder was present, so the scene can only be imagined.

What is known is that, with darkness falling, Tracy at last managed to throw the bloodhounds, Guard Carson, the possemen, and the reporters off his trail. Reluctantly, the pursuers called it a day and returned to Renton.

After supper two hours later, a logger named John Atwood, who had been working in the woods in the search area that afternoon, told a curious tale about an encounter he had had with Harry Tracy, whose identity he did not know at the time.

"He asked me if the logging road we were on led around the outskirts of Seattle," Atwood said, "saying he wanted to stay away from towns. I told him it did, though I wondered at the time why he wanted to avoid people. Now I know."

During this same session in a Renton saloon, the man the press had appropriately labeled a "galley slave," told his story. After disposing of a few drinks and a hearty meal provided by the newsmen, John Anderson, a recent immigrant of Scandanavian descent, told the following story in broken English:

> We left Port Madison on Saturday night at nine o'clock. We went to West Seattle and arrived at daylight. I pulled the boat. Tracy held a gun over me all the way. We landed south of the West Seattle elevator under a trestle, and went directly into the woods. We spent Sunday in the woods at West Seattle. When it got dark, we came across the bay in our boat, and landed at the sawmill at South Seattle. We then started on the railroad track toward Black River. We turned off the track to the left shortly before we reached Black River. We crossed a large hayfield and went into the woods. This was Monday morning. When we got into the timber, we cooked breakfast. We then rested until afternoon. At

three o'clock we started through the timber toward Renton.

Just before we reached the railroad bridge over Black River, we met four men, and Tracy said, "Hello, Fred," and jumped down to the bank to where the men were standing. Tracy talked to the men for a few minutes. After the talk, Tracy left one of the men to watch me. He and the three others, after blindfolding me, went off and stayed about an hour. When they returned, they brought a bottle of whiskey. Then we started out. Tracy forced me to walk in front, and he followed behind, accompanied by the four men we met on the bridge.

We arrived at Renton about eleven o'clock and walked up the railroad track through the town one and a half miles east of the brickyard. Here Tracy tied me up and he, accompanied by the four strange men, left me. They returned at daylight this morning and we went further back in the brush and cooked breakfast. After breakfast, Tracy told me he would go away for a while but would come back in an hour. When he returned, he brought the boy from the Gerrells' house, and we walked down to the Gerrells' place together. We were in the house about three hours when Tracy took me out to the chicken coop and said: "Lie down." After he tied me up, he cautioned me to keep still. I lay in this position until called to by Mrs. Gerrells, when I hobbled out into her backyard, where this gentleman (indicating a newspaper man) untied the leather straps which held my wrists.

Concluding what had been a long twenty-four hours for everybody concerned, the newsmen second-guessed the failures of the day, reaching the conclusion that two things had conspired to defeat the object of the chase: first, the late arrival of the posses from the sheriff's office; second, the failure of many of the men to obey orders, once they were stationed along the railroad track.

If the bloodhounds had been consulted, they might have pointed out two contributing factors—Tracy's unsportsman-like

use of cayenne pepper and taking a streetcar across an arm of
Lake Washington.

But they were not . . .

WHERE TRACY MADE HIS LATEST SENSATIONAL ESCAPE.

THE GERRELLS HOME, RENTON, WASH.

Seattle Post-Intelligencer
The Gerrell home, near Renton, Washington.

Newspaper clipping

Harry Tracy forced May Baker, right, Mrs. McKinney and her daughter, to accompany him to the Gerrell residence.

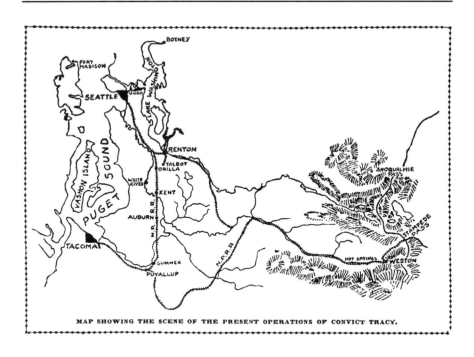

MAP SHOWING THE SCENE OF THE PRESENT OPERATIONS OF CONVICT TRACY.

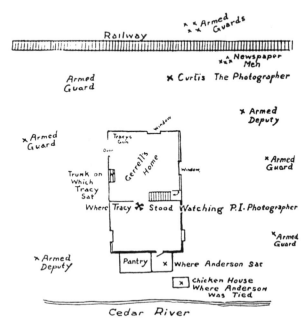

Chapter Nine
Is Tracy Insane?

TRACY LIES LOW

OUTLAW AGAIN COMPLETELY VANISHES

POSSE IS BADLY STUMPED

To all intents, Tracy, the outlaw, has disappeared from the face of the earth. All that the authorities can do is to wait until he enters another home or holds someone up. Rumors of the wildest description concerning the convict's whereabouts are flying around on all sides. Each coup the notorious murderer has made since his arrival in King County has been more spectacular than the last, and it is no exaggeration to say that the public expects his next exploit to surpass even his calcium-light performance at the Gerrells' home near Renton.

What the public could also expect from the press was more wild speculation on what Tracy had done or might do, based on interviews with people who had seen or *thought* they had seen Tracy or evidence that Tracy had passed by.

A theory that Tracy was insane gained credence. To prove it, several of his recent actions for which there was no other logical explanation were cited. For example, a man answering the description of Tracy had visited the home of C.B. Hillman, near Kenwood Station, at eight o'clock one night and asked to use the telephone. Mrs. Hillman was sitting near the telephone in the kitchen when the man pushed her aside and took down the receiver.

"Mrs. Hillman says he did not call for a number," a reporter wrote. "She went out front to see about her two-year-old baby, and the man followed her out and went down the street-car track toward Kenwood Station. When he came into the house, he was carrying a gun by the barrel, with the stock down. But when he left, he was carrying the gun under his arm, with the muzzle pointed to the ground."

If the man *was* Tracy, had that not been strange behavior? Or was it just a way for Mrs. Hillman to get her name in the paper?

Another inexplicable act by Harry Tracy, a reporter mused, was his visit to the Gerrells' home. He had not been hungry. He took nothing from the house. In fact, the only thing he did there was wash his face and hands, an act he could have performed just as well in any nearby creek. Well, yes, he did carry on a conversation with the three women, which might be an indication that he was lonely. But his giving Charles Gerrells two stolen pocket watches, telling him to sell them and use the proceeds to buy two revolvers and a supply of ammunition, sounded very odd.

"The murderer had friends near Renton who could have gotten the weapons for him," a reporter speculated. "He had parted with them only a few hours before he met the boy. Miss Baker says the outlaw really believed that Charles Gerrells would return with the revolvers until almost the time he left the house."

The fact that young Charles Gerrells betrayed him to the authorities rather than buying the revolvers was a serious breach of trust, Tracy must have felt, just as Mrs. Van Horn's revealing his presence to the grocery boy had been a few days earlier.

Was it possible, the reporter wondered, that Tracy's visit to the Gerrells' home was the fantasy of a disordered brain? Had the mental strain since his escape from prison proved too much for his iron nerves? Had he crossed the invisible line between sanity and insanity?

"In the excitement following Tracy's flight through the woods," the reporter wrote, "one important item was overlooked. He told Miss May Baker at the Gerrells' home that his real name was Harry Severn, and that Tracy was his criminal nom-de-plume. Whether the murderer was speaking the truth is a matter for speculation. He told the three women who were his unwilling companions many things which they were inclined to question. The conversation had been in a light vein when Miss Baker asked him to tell her his real name, and many believe that Tracy was speaking jestingly when he answered."

Meanwhile, the lack of tangible evidence regarding Tracy's whereabouts did not deter reporters from filling the papers with detailed stories of his alleged doings. According to one account, his former partner, David Merrill, still alive and well, was believed to have joined him near Renton and now was traveling with him.

"A man from the Salem penitentiary is authority for the statement," a reporter wrote. "It has been learned that Anderson's story regarding the four men whom Tracy met on Monday is absolutely correct. Merrill is one of these four men."

As to the other three men, a deputy sheriff not identified by the press captured three suspects near Renton the day after Tracy's escape. Though they looked like hobos, the deputy was sure that they were three of the four men who had met Tracy at the Black River bridge night before last.

"At the town jail they gave their names as Andy Nielson, Tom Madden, and Phil Ritchie. The first two say they are loggers, and the third says he is an iron bridge-builder. They say they came to Seattle a couple of days ago and went on a spree. A diligent search is being made for the fourth alleged accomplice, who is believed to be hanging around Renton."

By far the most interesting "Tracy-sighting" was attributed to a young lady of Miss May Baker's age, who, if not privileged to spend several hours in Tracy's presence, had imagination

enough to generate a full front-page column of fascinating copy
with no more evidence than a possibly stolen horse.

"The horse bearing the man supposed to be the convict was
seen by Miss Florence Williams," the account began, "sister of
City Attorney Sidney Williams of Renton, and Albert Sprague.
Mr. Sprague and Miss Williams were returning to Renton from
a drive in the country in a buggy."

Having established the credentials of the people willing to
vouch for the truth of the story, the reporter repeated what
Miss Williams had told him verbatim:

> *I had been watching the road ahead for several min-
> utes when I saw the outline of a white horse. The
> evening was growing very dark, and I could not see very
> plainly. Evidently the rider of the horse saw our buggy
> at the same time we looked at him, for he immediately
> turned the horse off the road into the brush along the
> roadside. I thought this act very suspicious. For that
> reason, I watched with closer interest. In the shadow of
> a large fence and half concealed by brush, I saw the
> man disappear over the side of the animal opposite us.
> We were close upon him then.*
>
> *As soon as we drove by the horse, I got a very good
> view of it, but could not see the man anywhere. The ani-
> mal was gray-coated, and of a little less than ordinary
> height. My suspicion of the man and his intentions
> grew more when I had seen the place where he had dis-
> mounted, for it was alongside a tall fence. There was no
> gate anywhere near the point, had he intended to enter
> the field and dismounted for that reason.*

Though the only solid facts established by the story told by
Miss Williams were that she had seen a horse, a man, and a
fence with no nearby gate, the credibility and the social standing of the witnesses inspired the reporter to hitch these facts to
several surmises and a few guesses, then hop into the vehicle
and ride it into the land of fancy.

> *The horse seen by the young couple answers in every
> way the description of an animal stolen from the*

pasture of John Mordich's farm Tuesday night. The general opinion is that should Tracy have ridden the horse up the road toward Seattle, he probably hid the animal in the woods before making toward the lake, as it is supposed he did. In that way, he could have thrown the hounds completely off the scent, reached water without undue fatigue, and been ready to approach Seattle from the east by way of the Lake Washington shore. The horse had not been found up to a late hour tonight.

Completing the story and justifying the logic was the news item:

Guard Carson, of Walla Walla, and Walter Lyon, of Salem, left here at four o'clock this afternoon, with the hounds, proceeding to Burrows' boathouse, where they expected the dogs would again take up the scent. But the brutes refused to work.

We can only wonder why. Were the bloodhounds saying that it was only people they tracked, not horses, boats, or fugitives walking in water? Or were their nostrils still smarting from the cayenne pepper?

Sent to Seattle by Oregon Governor Geer as his special representative in the Tracy manhunt, Walter Lyon, the Governor's private secretary, was a dog-lover, whose favorite breed was the bloodhound. Thanks to him, newspaper readers would learn a great deal about the Washington State Prison kennel and its tracking dogs.

Meeting the train from Walla Walla carrying Guard Carson and two willing young bloodhounds named Don and Bell, Walter Lyon introduced them to Sheriff Oscar H. Spencer and Deputy Sheriff Pennington, then took them to the county jail to wait until the whereabouts of their quarry could be ascertained. As noted earlier, Sheriff Cudihee had chartered the tugboat *Sea Lion*, whose captain was willing to take his possemen and the dogs anywhere they wanted to go on Puget Sound and the Strait of Juan de Fuca as soon as rumors of Tracy-sightings between the Pacific Ocean, the San Juan Islands, and British Columbia could be sorted out.

The dogs were in good condition and ready to go, the reporters were told. Both animals were young, about eighteen months old, with Don being much the bigger of the two.

"He is of a reddish-brown, or liver, color," a reporter wrote, "with a remarkably well shaped head. The veins are conspicuous, proving his breed to be excellent. He is of the old English bloodhound stock. On the other hand, Bell is of an entirely different strain, the Georgia Redbone stock, and is a black and tan. She was taken from a litter of pups but appears to be in fine fettle and will doubtless work as hard as Don."

Both bloodhounds had been acquired by the Walla Walla prison when very young, Walter Lyon learned, and now were part of a kennel containing twenty-one animals. Don had taken part in the chase twice—before and after it crossed the Columbia River. At that time, he and Hunter, his half-brother, worked under many disadvantages, Lyon said.

"They were hauled around in hacks under a burning sun, and worked in the dust until they gave out completely and lay down on the trail. Don has recuperated and is again in good condition, but Hunter snagged his right hind leg a few days ago and could not be brought over."

It was the intention, Lyon said, to bring along Old Bess, the keenest bloodhound in the pack, but she was in poor condition and might die because of her mistreatment while hunting Tracy and Merrill in Oregon.

"She was allowed to get overheated after trailing the convicts a long distance," he told a reporter indignantly, "and then was plunged into a cold river. Don and Bell are both first-class hounds, Guard Carson tells me, and I believe good work may be expected of them. Bell has never been engaged in an actual manhunt, but her training has been as good as that of Don. I feel confident that they will make a good showing, if given the proper opportunity."

A night or two later, another Tracy-sighting was reported by two young women who lived in the Auburn area, who said they were sure they had seen the phantom-like figure as he passed them on a country road.

"Both young women claim that Tracy was carrying his rifle in his right trousers leg when he passed them, the stock only being visible at the waist line."

Apparently well aware that carrying a gun in this manner would make a quick-draw rather awkward, Tracy attempted to remedy that situation early the next morning when he showed up at the home of still another Swedish immigrant, E.M. Johnson, and demanded his aid in acquiring more appropriate weapons.

"Tracy seems to have a predilection for people named Johnson," a reporter noted. "He made Louis B. Johnson, of Bothell, drive him from that place to Woodland Park, after killing Deputy Sheriff Raymond at Wayne. At Port Madison, he entered the home of John Johnson and decamped with Anderson, the hired man. After leaving the Gerrells' home at Renton, he fled to the house of Kent Johnson."

Of course in the Puget Sound region at that time, the woods were full of Scandinavian immigrants, inspiring a bit of popular doggerel:

A thousand Swedes ran through the weeds,
Chasing a wild Norwegian . . .

Or was it the other way round?

At any rate, this particular Swede was as badly frightened as any newcomer to America could be, for Harry Tracy, hurt and angry from his recent betrayal by Charles Gerrells and Mrs. Van Horn, was in an ugly mood. In English so broken, the reporter could barely understand him, Johnson said:

> *He told me he was Tracy when he came through the front door with a rifle in his hand. He first demanded something to eat. After my wife had cooked him his breakfast, he told me he wanted firearms and more ammunition. He gave me to understand that his gun was loaded, and if I did not go to Tacoma and procure him two .45-caliber revolvers and 100 rounds of ammunition, he would murder my wife and children.*
>
> *I told him I did not have any money. He then said I had better go to Kent and borrow it, and then get the*

first train for Tacoma. I was afraid that if I did not do as I was told he would kill my family, and I hurried to Kent and secured some money from a friend and took the 7 o'clock train. In Tacoma I found that I had only money enough to buy one gun. I returned to Kent about 4 o'clock. When I reached home, I found my wife was in a state of nervous collapse from fright. I gave Tracy the gun and ammunition and he seemed pleased.

Shortly after my arrival, he ordered my wife to cook him a supply of food to last a week. She boiled about two dozen eggs and gave him plenty of flour and sugar. He asked for a sack, and placed the provisions in it. He remained about the house until dark, and then took his departure down the road on one of my horses. I found the animal today. It was dark, and I cannot say which way he went. Once he asked the easiest way to reach Seattle. He also spoke about Auburn. He appeared to be very uneasy, and after I returned made several trips into the yard and looked about to see if any person was approaching.

From his actions, I believe he thought he was being pursued. During the afternoon, my folks say he took up a position on a hill just in the rear of my house and watched the road. He seemed to be completely exhausted, and I don't think he has had any sleep since he left Seattle and vicinity.

I often wanted to attack him while he was at the house, but was afraid he would kill some member of my family if I did so. He did not give me any opportunity to get hold of his rifle. Besides the gun I bought for him, he had his rifle and an old gun with a black stock. It looked like an Army revolver. He told me it was not good for very much, and he wanted to get rid of it. He carried a revolver in each hip pocket when he left the house and his rifle under his arm. His coat, vest and trousers are black, the trousers being too short.

When Tracy first came to the house and stated who he was, my wife and I told him we would do anything he asked us. He did not seem to pay attention to what we said, but began to give orders at once. I am so afraid that he will pay a second visit to our house that I have deserted it, and will not return until he has been located.

Whether Tracy himself or a prankster pretending to be the outlaw phoned the office of Sheriff Cudihee in Seattle that afternoon, taunting the sheriff and inviting him to come pay a social call, though not revealing his location, would remain an unsolved mystery. Not so mysterious, though also unsolved, was a problem that had arisen down in Salem, Oregon. An article in the *Oregonian* asked which government entity should pay for the pursuit of Tracy and Merrill?

"'Who shall foot the bill?' is the question now before the authorities. The county is asked to pay the expenses on the theory that the chase was for two murderers who had committed crimes in Marion County, and were wanted to answer for their acts. Marion County will take the view that Tracy and Merrill were escaped convicts; that they were pursued as such, and that the expenses should be paid out of the state appropriation for that purpose.

Sheriff Durbin pointed out that prison Superintendent Lee "told me to spare no expense in capturing the men, who were committed to the State Prison for safe-keeping. If they escaped, the state should pay for their re-capture."

Furthermore, the sheriff said, he was out considerable money advanced by him to pay incidental expenses. The total cost for the militia was about $700, and for the posse $260, and this does not include any compensation for the time of the men composing the posse.

For the present, at least, Sheriff Cudihee was not arguing with King County or the State of Washington about the money he was spending on the Tracy chase. But to make the search more effective, he decided to reduce his forces, though he vowed to "continue the hunt as long as the fugitive remains in Washington."

By now, the sheriff was pretty sure that Harry Tracy had plunged into the thick undergrowth of Ginter Swamp, southeast of the town of Black Diamond, for the bloodhounds had tracked him that far until losing the trail in water and darkness. All kinds of wild rumors were circulating.

"At one time, the report was started that a battle had been fought, resulting in the death of seven deputies and the wounding of the convict."

When the grains of fact had been separated from the chaff of fiction, it was learned that four deputies had fired a total of sixteen shots in uncertain light at a man assumed to be Tracy, who had fired back. None of the deputies had been hit, but the man assumed to be Tracy was assumed to have been wounded because "All the deputies who engaged in this encounter are good marksmen . . ."

The next confirmed Tracy-sighting was by a stump-rancher named Frank Pautot, who lived in the woods near Black Diamond. For the reader unfamilar with the term "stump-rancher," a pioneer in that place and time who filed a land claim in the Puget Sound area usually encountered such a thick growth of big trees on his land that he had to fell a number of them in order to let enough sunlight reach the ground to permit him to build a cabin, plant a vegetable garden, and fence a pasture large enough to graze a few milk cows, work oxen, and horses. Often the 200-foot tall trees were chopped or sawed at head-level, leaving a five-foot stump that could only be disposed of by burning during the dry summer months, a process that took weeks. So when a settler was asked what he was raising on his claim, he often answer sardonically, "Stumps. Got a ranch full of 'em."

At six o'clock, the night before, Frank Pautot told a reporter next day, he saw a stranger coming through the woods toward his house. Brandishing a rifle, the man approached to within twenty feet, then said he was Harry Tracy and wanted supper.

"He ordered the old man into the house," the reporter wrote, "where Mrs. Pautot was preparing the evening meal. The convict sat down, and said he was very hungry and tired. He rolled up his right trousers leg and exposed a very badly swollen limb.

He complained of rheumatism, and said the recent wet nights had about done him up."

While eating and looking out the kitchen window, Tracy saw Deputy Sheriff Fred Berner coming up the road. Believing that the officer was leading a posse, Tracy jumped up from his chair, drew a revolver, and, with it in his left hand and the rifle in his right, ordered the couple into the bedroom, while he remained standing and looking out the window.

"Deputy Berner, followed by several of his posse, was hurrying on to Black Diamond," the reporter wrote. "The men all passed the house without inquiring about Tracy. Pautot said Tracy could hardly walk, and that he had commanded him to procure a horse and drive him to Buckley, near Orting, in Pierce County. Mr. Pautot said the desperado remained in the house until nearly dark, and left after threatening the couple with murder if they came from their house that night and told of his presence there."

When informed of the incident, Sheriff Cudihee became convinced that the reason Tracy was headed for Buckley was because he had decided to hop on a Northern Pacific train headed east across the Cascades.

> The theory on which the officers are working is that Tracy is trying to reach a point near Buckley where the grade is very steep in order to board a freight train. He evidenced his intentions to get east of the Cascades at the Green River Bridge, between Covington and Auburn, but was unable to get aboard the train. The conductor of a freight train perceived the convict trying to swing on to the caboose at the end of the train. He was clearly visible in the light of the lantern on the rear platform, and was seen to drop his pack. When the train passed him, he returned and picked the pack up.

Although all law enforcement officers, including railroad "bulls," had been alerted to Tracy's presence in the area and had vowed to take him dead or alive because he had killed several of their kind, there was good reason to believe that train crews were sympathetic toward the outlaw. During the past decade, agitators for the Industrial Workers of the World, the

I.W.W., (sometimes called the "Wobblies" or the "I Won't Work's,") had advocated war without quarter between Capital and Labor, gaining many adherents among loggers, miners, and railway workers. All authority was resented by its members. If Harry Tracy attempted to swing aboard a slow-moving freight car as it climbed a steep grade, a badge-carrying railroad bull might club him over the head and knock him loose from his hold on the iron rung of the car's ladder. But a brakeman or switchman would reach down and give him a hand up.

"A circumstance which has provoked much indignation," a reporter wrote, "is the outspoken sentiment of a certain train crew which daily encounters fugitives along the route. Almost to a man, this crew has expressed itself in language which leaves little doubt in the minds of many that Convict Tracy would be a welcome guest across the Cascade Mountains."

Sheriff Cudihee has called in the posse looking for Convict Tracy, and now proposes to surprise Tracy and Merrill when they shall meet again. Tracy was seen by a farmer near Enumclaw Sunday night, but his appearance was not reported until yesterday. The fugitive played his old trick of doubling on his tracks and again his pursuers were fooled. He was not heard from yesterday. Merrill is said to be in Seattle, and has even ventured out on the streets.

Though no reliable witness had actually seen David Merrill, Sheriff Cudihee assumed that he was still around, just as he assumed that Harry Tracy had been so seriously wounded that his movements were now restricted.

"Sheriff Cudihee is preparing for a long vigil," a reporter wrote on July 15, "founded on the belief that buckshot wounds in his body have transformed Harry Tracy from a veritable winged traveler into a cunning, desperate man, who must now use his wits rather than his legs for safety."

At the same time, the sheriff admitted that the area in which Tracy was last seen offered many ideal hiding places, where a fugitive need not do much running to evade capture.

"He was seen this morning on a road near the Muckelshoot reservation by an Indian boy," a reporter wrote. "But tracking him there will be difficult, for hundreds of paths run through the tall timber and dense underbrush. Even the oldest inhabitants know little about these trails, and but a small number of the Indians on the reservation are well acquainted with their tortuous courses."

Since the Muckelshoot Indians were one of a number of Puget Sound tribes which, not too many years ago, had been forced to sign treaties confining them to small reservations in poor country, where they now eked out a meager existence as virtual prisoners in a land where they once roamed free, it was not likely that an Indian would give the fugitive up to the law. Certainly, as experienced hunters, none of them would be so foolish as to pursue a wounded, armed man known to be a deadly shot into his refuge, no matter what the promised reward.

Meanwhile, down in Oregon, Governor Geer was receiving all sorts of suggestions and proposals from people regarding the capture, punishment, or pardon of Tracy and Merrill. Of particular interest was one purporting to come from H.T. Turner, president of the Seattle Hygienic Sanitarium, which said:

> The so-called outlaw, Harry Tracy, has conducted himself in and around Seattle so as to have won the sympathy of the great mass of thoughtful people. On every side we hear the expression: "Tracy is a brick, he is a jewel. A man with his abilities should not be hunted by bloodhounds and bounty-seekers."
>
> Why not issue an edict of pardon for him and place him in some responsible position where his qualifications and abilities can be put to use for the benefit of humanity? He will appreciate the position and opportunity, and that big heart of his, and great soul, would be a great benefit to the race, perhaps as a detective.

The letter went on to say that since Tracy had gotten the rifle used during his escape from a prison guard, all the men he had killed had been in self-defense. The governor was advised that if he withdrew the reward offer and issued a pardon, he would achieve immortality. "Every great man has but one opportunity to do a universal good to his fellow men. This is, I believe, your great opportunity."

For some reason, Governor Geer did not respond.

N. TUESDAY. JULY 8. 1902.- FOURTEEN PAGES.

TRAIL OF TRACY VANISHES IN AIR

IS NOT FOUND IN KITSAP COUNTY

Clews Followed Since His Departure From Port Madison Lead to Nothing----Johnsons Boat and Hired Man Are Still Missing ----Pursuit Is Now in Suspense

TRACY, THE OUTLAW DISAPPEARS

SINCE Tracy, the escaped convict, left the Johnson home at Port Madison absolutely no clew has been discovered as to his whereabouts. Forty Indians are watching for the murderer in Kitsap county. The coast of the whole lower Sound is being patrolled. Guards are lying in ambush on the approaches to Bothell. The authorities are waiting for the next appearance of the convict. They can make no move until he again shows himself. For the time being Tracy has vanished as completely as if swallowed by the earth.

The bloodhounds from the Walla Walla penitentiary arrived last night at 9 o'clock. They came to Seattle too late to be taken to Port Madison as at first intended. Unless the murderer bobs up again in Kitsap county, the hounds will not be taken to Port Madison. The tug Sea Lion has been under steam all night, ready to leave at a moment's notice, with the animals on board. She was prepared to leave for any place on Puget Sound where the criminal might put in an appearance. Never since Tracy escaped from the Salem penitentiary have the officers of the law been so eager for the chase. Sheriff Cudihee will return from Port Madison this morning, where he went yesterday in a launch.

Investigation yesterday showed that the reports of Tracy's presence in Kitsap county were unfounded. The man seen by the Indian woman of the Fort Madison reservation proved to be a crippled beachcomber. He carried a rifle and in several ways bore a slight resemblance to the murderer. He has been on the beach for some time. The report that a woman was held up ten miles beyond Sidney by a man resembling Tracy turned out to be fiction. The story was based on the fact that a logger without money had appeared at a house and asked for a meal. He was returning to his camp from Seattle. The boat found on the beach at Miller's bay belonged to a rancher named Samuel Horsley. It had not been moved from its position.

Beyond guarding the different points threatened by Tracy, and waiting for his next appearance, the authorities of the different counties on the Sound have no definite plans. They are running each report down and looking for facts.

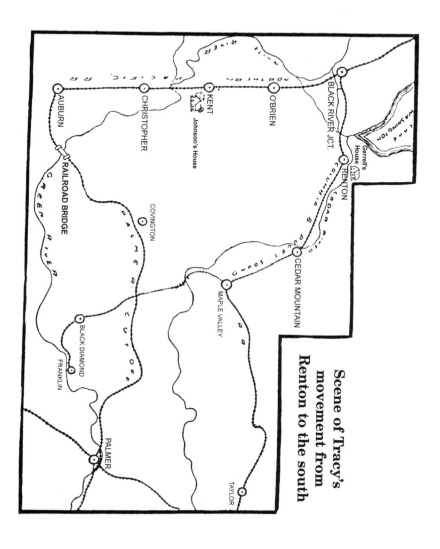

Scene of Tracy's
movement from
Renton to the south

CHAPTER TEN
HEADLINE HUNTERS

In a more enlightened age—say a hundred years later—most all the people involved in the Harry Tracy saga would have gotten their fourteen minutes of fame in the form of made-for-TV-movies, tabloid payments, or paperback book contracts. But considering the lack of modern-day communication techniques, the local media did not do too badly, as the ads on the facing page illustrate:

How many lots were sold in the housing development on Green Lake by the use of Tracy's name or how many grade school children showed their envious friends the grimy little palm that had shook the hand of the galley slave who had rowed Tracy's boat, has not been recorded for posterity. But in that place and time, the event probably would compare with receiving a hand-written thank-you note from Ken Griffey, Jr. for returning the baseball he hit into your lap the day he broke all existing homerun records.

Although the Swedish hired hand, John Anderson, did not speak English very well and was a newcomer to the United States, he understood the language and the system well enough to give colorful interviews when questioned by officers or reporters. Called upon to identify articles taken by Tracy from the Johnson's Port Madison home, he recognized the stolen satchel and several well-fried pancakes, which had become so hard that the fleeing convict had abandoned them. Anderson also demonstrated his sense of humor by saying that he had lived so long on Tracy's cooking he almost hated to make a change. He did manage, however, to do justice to the hearty meals prepared for him at the county jail where he was taken for questioning. The *Post Intelligencer* reported:

> *Probably no man read with more interest the* Post-Intelligencer's *complete account of Tracy's doings of Tuesday than Anderson. He smiled when he noticed his likeness on the front page and stated that if he had been prepared for a picture he would have tried to look a little better. He scanned the columns closely and when he came to some part he couldn't exactly understand he sought assistance from Night Jailer Huney.*

Sparing no expense in its effort to secure the best-quality photos that could be taken with the equipment then available, the *P-I* sent Ashael Curtis, who, with his brother Edward were the finest photographers in the Pacific Northwest, to photograph and interview the Kent rancher, E.M. Johnson, whom Tracy had forced to take an early-morning train to Tacoma and buy him a revolver.

After hitching up his team for the day's work, Johnson told Curtis, he went into the house to get breakfast. As he sat down, a man entered without knocking, then said:

"I suppose you know who I am."

"I guess I do. You're Tracy."

"Then you know the fix I'm in."

"Yes, I do," Johnson said, vainly trying to swallow his food. "And you can have anything you want."

Tracy stood by the fire and warmed himself, Johnson told Curtis, then asked for a change in clothing. Though she was very nervous and excited, Mrs. Johnson went into the bedroom, opened a bureau drawer, then returned with an armload of underclothing, turning her back as Tracy stripped, dried himself, and changed.

After eating a hearty breakfast, Tracy told Johnson he wanted him to go to Tacoma and buy two .45-caliber revolvers. Tracy started to make a list of what he wanted, but changed his mind and said:

"Write it down yourself."

"But I am a poor talker, I cannot write at all, and I have no money."

"Well, write it down the best you can. If you don't have any money, borrow it from somebody, because if you don't get the guns for me before noon and come back alone, I'll kill your wife and children."

Johnson borrowed forty dollars from a banker friend in Kent without telling him what it was for, caught the seven o'clock train to Tacoma, and bought one revolver, being unable to obtain another for reasons he hoped he could explain to Tracy later.

Meanwhile, Mrs. Johnson was so concerned for the safety of her seventeen-year-old daughter Annie, and her fifteen-year-old son, Lars, because of the threat Tracy had made to kill all the members of the family if her husband did not return with the revolvers by noon, that she began to plead for the lives of her children, saying she was willing to pay the penalty if her husband did not get back by then, but she begged him to spare the children.

"Have you ever heard of me doing anything bad to women and children?" Tracy demanded, looking hurt.

"Well, no—"

"Just read the Seattle *Post-Intelligencer* story on how I treated the Gerrells family, if you think I would ever hurt women and children."

"I know you treated them well, Mr. Tracy. But I'm afraid you'll hurt my husband or take him away with you when you leave."

"The only reason I might hurt your husband, Mrs. Johnson, would be if he brings deputies back with him. If he does that, I'll kill him—and them, too. If they start shooting at me, you and the children had better find trees to hide behind. Because when the fighting starts, Tracy never runs."

When her husband did not come home on the noon train, Mrs. Johnson told Tracy that the next train would be at 4 p.m. She was sure her husband would be on it. Saying he would not harm her and the children before then, Tracy and the Johnson family spent most of the morning and early afternoon hours on a hilltop overlooking the house and the railroad tracks, waiting.

During that time, Mrs. Johnson told a reporter later, Tracy talked a great deal, telling a number of stories about his recent experiences and his crime-filled life.

"I feel sorry that I had to hold the Gerrells family," he said. "I enjoyed my visit very much. Anderson told a lot of lies about how I treated him. I did tie him. It was necessary. I did not strike or kick him, however, and did not hold a gun on him while he was rowing me in the boat." Falling silent for a moment, Tracy muttered grimly, "I'll surely kill him. He tells too many lies."

During one phase of his career, Tracy told Mrs. Johnson, he had robbed five banks in quick succession with the help of two accomplices, netting a total of $36,000.

"But I had to give up my share," he sighed, "in order to protect my pals. Later, an innocent man was sent to the penitentiary for thirty-five years—convicted of a crime of which he knew nothing."

Taking a liking to Annie Johnson, described by a reporter as "a vivacious girl of more than ordinary conversational powers," Tracy complained to her bitterly that the possemen were pursuing him only for the rewards.

"They will get $5,000 if they capture me alive," he said, "and $8,500 if they kill me."

Truth was, Mrs. Johnson admitted later, her only bad moments with Tracy came when she worried about what he would do if her husband failed to carry out his instructions. Otherwise, he was very well-mannered.

"When it came time to eat, I told him that I hated to build a fire on such a warm day. He told me not to bother about it, saying that a cold lunch was good enough. He asked me if I had any strawberries in the house. I told him that I had some canned berries, and would open a jar for him. He said he had not had any for five years. He ate two large dishes with great relish."

When her husband came walking up the hill toward the house after getting off the four o'clock train, Mrs. Johnson was relieved to see that he was alone. Tracy was so eager to inspect the package he was carrying that he sent her son running down to get it and bring it back to the house. Though it contained only one revolver and a box of cartridges, Tracy fondled the weapon with pleasure, exclaiming:

"This is just what I wanted!"

When her husband came into the house a few moments later, Tracy asked why he had brought back only one revolver, when he had been instructed to purchase two.

"You told me not to buy more than one gun at any one store," Johnson said. "When I went to the second place, they did not have the kind that was ordered. But to show you I am honest, here is the money the other one would have cost."

"I don't want your money," Tracy said. "You did just right. Don't worry about it. But I will take three dollars from you as a loan."

"No, take it all. There's about twenty dollars here."

"All right, I'll take it. But just as a loan, mind you. Money is of no use to me, really. And the only reason I want revolvers is to protect myself."

When Tracy left, he did not force her to give him food, Mrs. Johnson said. "I volunteered to give him what I had. He indicated with a finger where I should cut the ham. I filled a baking powder can with butter, gave him three loaves of bread, and a cup of salt. The salt was put up at his suggestion. He explained that he might find it handy in the timber, where if he ran short of food he could use it in seasoning any grouse he might shoot."

Before leaving, Tracy asked Mrs. Johnson if she could give him a few sheets of writing paper, some envelopes, and stamps. She gave him two envelopes and a couple of two-cent stamps, but did not have any writing paper.

"Before he left, Tracy shook hands with all of us," Johnson said. "He took a white horse, and stated that he would turn him loose about a mile down the road after he had struck the brush. The horse came home during the night.

"Tracy did not joke any at my house. Twice he talked about his mother, and I could see tears in his eyes each time. He told me that when he went to a house he always tried to pick out one owned by poor people, as they thought more of their family than rich people, and he not only liked their society, but was surer of forcing a compliance with his orders."

Ironically, Tracy's method of persuading people to do what he wanted usually worked better than means used by lawmen to persuade civilian cooperation. A case in point was a Tracy-sighting by a young farmer named Michael Dolan, who, while driving toward town with a wagon load of vegetables, saw a man he thought was Tracy dozing in thick brush cover near the Green River bridge. Hoping he had not been seen, Dolan drove on down the road until he met a farmer friend named George Hummel, to whom he exclaimed excitedly:

"Go into town as fast as you can and tell the posse there that Tracy is now lying in the brush just across the bridge. He has been there since noon. Don't give me away on this, as it might get to Tracy's ears, and then I would be afraid to stay around here any longer."

Whipping his team into a run, Hummel drove into town, where he told Sheriff Zimmerman the news he had been asked to relay. Unfortunately, there were no posses around at the moment, the nearest one being with Sheriff Cudihee in Puyallup, too many miles away in the wrong direction to be of any use.

"Notifying the sheriff's office in Seattle by phone of what he had learned and his intended action, Sheriff Zimmerman procured a horse and buggy and with a staff correspondent for the *Post-Intelligencer* (a requirement for the chase scenes), drove at a fast clip to the Dolan ranch."

Dolan was not there at the moment, having gone to a neighbor's place half a mile away to give a man named Neely a hand. The sheriff and the reporter drove there, found Michael Dolan, and asked him to tell them what he knew. He was very reluctant to do so. Shifting uneasily from one foot to another, gazing first at the ground and then at his interrogators, he finally blurted:

"Say, are you sure I'm not going to get into trouble with Tracy if I tell you anything?"

When the exasperated sheriff assured Michael Dolan that he was going to have big trouble with *him* if he didn't tell what he knew, the young vegetable farmer talked freely enough, giving the details of where and when he had seen the man he thought to be Tracy. Tooling the buggy in that direction as fast as he could drive it, Sheriff Zimmerman, aided by the *P-I* reporter, searched for Tracy's sign, but found none.

Driving back down the road at a slower pace, they encountered James Dolan, father of the young man who had reported the sighting. Though he knew the elder Dolan to be a rather crabby individual, Sheriff Zimmerman showed him his badge, then asked if he had any information regarding the Tracy sighting. The *P-I* reporter faithfully recorded the ensuing dialog.

"Supposing I do know something?" asked the old man. "What's in it for me if I tell?"

"What!" ejaculated the astonished official. "Do you mean to say that with a murderous villain like Tracy wandering around the country, killing people and tying others, you would want money to give information assisting in his capture? Why, man, Tracy might select you as the next person to rob, bind, and gag. He might even impress you into his service as he did Anderson."

"Well, what's that to you? You live by your brains, don't you? So do I. I know where Tracy is, but I would not tell you now if you gave me a gold mine."

The fires of Zimmerman's indignation leaped into vigorous flame, (the reporter wrote). In expressing his opinion of Dolan, he used language that would not look well in print. Fearing personal violence, Dolan took to his heels and ran down the road as fast as his legs could carry him.

"That man's cupidity and effrontery fairly paralyze me," exclaimed Zimmerman as he drove on. "A few more men like that in this state, and Tracy never would be caught."

On July 16, 1902, the following headlines appeared in all the Seattle and Portland papers:

MERRILL IS DEAD

Tracy Killed His Pal,
Just as He Said.

Brother of Outlaw
Identifies the Remains.

According to a syndicated report in the Chehalis, Wash. newspaper:

All doubt of Convict Harry Tracy's story that he had slain his pal, David Merrill was removed today by the news that Merrill's dead body had been found four miles southeast of here, partially concealed by two logs, between which the murderer had thrown it.

Accompanying the account was a four-column photo of Mrs. Mary Waggoner, looking grim and solemn in a long black dress, and her twelve-year son, George Waggoner, trying to look manly as he held a short-barreled rifle, stock down, standing grim and solemn beside her. Mother and son had been picking wild blackberries in the woods near the Northern Pacific railroad track, the story said, when a bad odor in a nearby thicket led them to the decomposed body. Thinking at once of the accounts they had been reading about Tracy and Merrill, they investigated and made their find.

The body was lying between two logs, face down, with the legs and one hand up. The spot where it lay is about two hundred feet from the Northern Pacific track, on an unfrequented road, and so distant from any dwelling that the crack of Tracy's murderous rifle might have sounded without attracting any attention.

The place where the body was found and the location of the bullet holes corroborated the story Tracy had told the crew aboard the gasoline launch that had carried him from Olympia to Seattle several weeks earlier. Angered by learning from a Portland newspaper he had read in a settler's cabin just north of Vancouver that David Merrill had been responsible for his capture three years ago, Tracy decided to get rid of Merrill, proposing a duel in which each man would walk ten paces, then turn and fire. In one account, he said he had turned after the eighth step; in another, after the ninth. Three bullets from his .30-.30-caliber Winchester rifle struck Merrill, one in the middle of the back, a second in the left side, and the third, fired at close range, though the head.

Before revealing the news to the press, Warden J.T. Janes of the state penitentiary in Salem, Oregon, was sent for, as was Ben Merrill, the dead man's brother, who currently was working at a sawmill in Chehalis, to give positive identification of the remains. Only after both men had done so was the news released.

Further investigation among residents of the area brought out the fact that the nearest neighbor to the site was a Bohemian named Frank Vrba and his wife, who lived about three hundred yards south of where the killing happened. A reporter wrote:

> *Mr. Vrba, who does not speak English, told the Sheriff in German that two weeks ago last Saturday (June 28) at 5:20 o'clock in the morning two men passed his house walking on the road. He was about one hundred feet from them, and did not know whether they saw him or not. He described one of the men as having on a black coat with blue trousers and a dark hat, and said the other had on a solid blue Army suit. One carried a rifle on his shoulder, and the other had one over his arm. Mrs. Vrba, who was in the milkhouse, also saw the men, but neither heard any shots.*

On that same day, a neighbor called old man Porter said his house was robbed, which angered him so much that, after seeing where one of the thieves had changed clothing, he had put his hounds on their trail, which the dogs followed to the south bank of the Newaukum River. It was just a mile or so north of here that Merrill's remains were found.

When Prison Superintendent Lee was asked if the discovers of the fugitive's body would be given the reward offered by the State of Oregon, he equivocated:

> *The reward will be paid according to the language of the offer, which was for the 'capture and return' of the convicts, dead or alive. In any event, we will pay liberally for the return of the body, even though it was not captured as specified in the offer.*

Now that it was established that David Merrill was dead, the press began to criticize Sheriff Edward Cudihee for his lack of diligence in catching a lone fugitive whose hunt had now encompassed five weeks, three hundred miles, and the efforts of hundreds of men. Headlines read:

CUDIHEE ON STILL HUNT

SHERIFF PURSUING OUTLAW TRACY DROPS OUT OF SIGHT.

Almost Every Effort Exhausted to Locate the Officer—No sign of the Fugitive.

Sheriff Cudihee is undoubtedly on a still-hunt after Convict Tracy. He has proved himself to be Tracy's equal in the matter of sudden disappearances, and neither the newspapermen nor the remaining members of the old posse have so far been able to locate him.

It was generally believed, the aggrieved reporter continued, that the sheriff and gone into hiding and taken a stand in the deep woods southeast of Seattle along unfrequented backroads or trails over which Tracy might be expected to pass if and when he tried to cross the Cascades toward eastern Washington.

Certainly, his appearance east of the mountains was anticipated by law officers there, for a news story from North Yakima dated July 16 read:

It is known here that Sheriff Tucker late this afternoon received a communication which had direct connection with the chase after Tracy. Two strangers, who kept well away from the public, were in town from the west side of the Cascades. Seven deputies have this evening been seen about the Sheriff's office. It is certain that preparations are being made to meet Tracy in case he should come over the mountains.

Speculating that if Tracy crossed the mountains by the most convenient route, Stampede Pass, he would have to catch a train to do so, for a man on foot or riding a horse could not go through the seven-mile-long railroad tunnel. Complaining that the authorities were conspiring against reporters like himself, this one wrote plaintively:

> *In light of the new system of the authorities in keeping from the press the information most wanted by the public, the reticence of the local authorities is deemed significant. Every door is closed.*

Since Sheriff Cudihee could not be found and no other law officers would tell the press what was going on, this particular reporter felt it his right to offer his personal critique of the bogged-down manhunt.

> *Without question, the chase is not being prosecuted vigorously enough. Without question, there has been a lack of generalship. Without question, the Sheriff's deputies ought to have killed Tracy in the first battle; they ought to have killed him at the Van Horn residence; they ought to have shot him down before he could have taken a boat at Meadow Point for Port Madison; they ought to have killed him many times over at the Gerrells' residence; they ought never to have permitted him to escape from the railroad cut several nights ago; and they ought to have trapped him at the Pautot house the day following.*

No doubt many of the city-dwelling readers at whom the reporter's strong rhetoric was aimed thought this great stuff. But a more thoughtful rural reader might have asked: "Why didn't one of the reporters who had a clear shot at Harry Tracy bring him down?"

Another thoughtful reader might have suggested that loading a carryall with amateur possemen and trigger-happy reporters, then tooling cross-country in a cloud of dust, was "like hunting ducks with a brass band." Many rural readers accustomed to filling their larders with deer, elk, and other wild game meat might have pointed out that, while charging a herd of buffalo on an open plain on horseback with a large party of men shooting at random was one way to down game, still-hunting by a single man who picked his spot, then spent end-less hours patiently waiting for his quarry to pass his way, could be even more effective, not to mention being much cheap-er so far as effort and expense were concerned.

During the lull in the Tracy hunt, regional newspaper writ-ers tried to satisfy reader demand for interesting copy by exploring the feelings of persons affected by the killings. A columnist wrote:

> *The skill which Tracy shows in eluding his pursuers has caused the expression of considerable sympathy for him. Utterances of admiration for his qualities are heard on every hand. It is true that the ingenuity, brav-ery and decisive action in the presence of mortal danger which have been displayed by the fugitive convict are such as to elict wonder. But admiration for Tracy's hardihood and cunning should not be permitted to out-weigh the heinousness of his crimes.*
>
> *There was no sympathy for Tracy at Salem Thursday when the body of Merrill was delivered. The only solemnity there was caused by a recollection of the sorrow that had been brought to three Salem homes by Merrill and his fellow-conspirator in murder. The many friends of the slain guard, Frank Ferrell, remem-bered him as good-hearted, cheerful, and generous, yet he had been shot down without warning, leaving his wife alone, desolate, and so ill at this time that her sur-vival is doubtful.*
>
> *The widow and eight children of Guard S.R.T. Jones are now without means of support, and Mrs. B.F. Tiffany is left in her grief with only a small amount of money saved by her husband. The remembrance of the happy homes broken and the honest, industrious men slain, dispelled every feeling of sympathy for Merrill in his death by treachery. There was more of rejoicing than sorrow when his remains were brought back to the prison to be buried.*

In the Seattle area, too, there was sadness, the columnist continued, for three good men who were only doing their duty had been killed by Harry Tracy.

All of these murdered men and bereaved families owe their tragic fate to the human hyena whose cruelty spared them not, though they had never harmed him in any way. He even turned basely on the companion of his wanderings and shot him in the back, proving that for him at least there is no truth in the old belief in honor among thieves.

There is not a more execrable wretch on earth than this miscreant Tracy, who has outraged every honorable sentiment of the heart and declared himself outside the pale of natural morality. There is an unwritten code in every human breast that teaches us not to take up arms against the innocent; not to betray a companion in danger; not to bring needless suffering upon those who have never harmed us. Tracy has forfeited the last particle of respect. He is the mortal enemy of the human race. The world will be better and the Pacific Coast more honorable the sooner he is killed like the wild beast he is.

In Salem, Oregon, that same day, a story noted:

The body of David Merrill was buried in the prison graveyard, without prayers, tears or regrets. A loathsome thing, scarcely recognizable as the medium through which many dark and bloody crimes were committed, the only thought after identification was to get the body out of sight under four full feet of earth. The events of the past month indicate that Merrill was the tool, as later he was the victim, of Tracy, and this permits a margin of pity for him, which, however, does not extend to regret for his death or the manner of it. Having lived in defiance of the law, he died as the fool dieth, and was buried as the carcass of a brute is buried, to save the world a nuisance.

Because of the continuing interest in the Tracy story, the *Oregonian* had sent one of its top writers, a man identified only by the initials "J.J.M." to Seattle for the duration of the man-hunt. With little hard news to report and no local editor to blue-pencil his copy, he felt free to make comments on the local citizens and their behavior so caustic that his articles probably would have cost him his job if written about the people at home. On July 22, he wrote:

> *While Seattle is not suffering from Tracy-itis in the acute form that manifested itself a week ago, the fragments and snatches of news that drift in from the front every few hours still draw crowds to the bulletin boards. The newspapers, having retired the outlaw to an inside page, still put flaring headlines over him. Frantic citizens of this strenuous town open their papers and turn to the Tracy page the first thing. Women who ordinarily rivet their earliest attention to the department store advertisements, now give Tracy first choice, while strong and presumably rational men, who have used Tracy news once, now use no other.*

Tracy's success in continuing to elude capture would have a negative effect on Sheriff Cudihee's chances for re-election, J.J.M. reported. Coming to Seattle from the wild and woolly mining town of Leadville, Colorado, "where men go around with pistols in their belts and kill people in order to keep up the reputation of the town," Cudihee had brought along a reputation for always getting his man. When he went after Tracy, the public assumed that if any law officer could capture Tracy, he would.

> *People were beginning to plan a grand legal hanging to add to the gaiety of the town, cutting Oregon out of the chance to punish her star offender. Poor Cudihee! He's become a mental and physical wreck, racing around like a blinded bull, chasing this way and that, ready to shoot at his own shadow, while the good people of Seattle swear that at the next election they will have a sheriff who can arrest something beside deserted cabins.*

Out in the suburbs, business had come to a standstill, J.J.M. wrote tongue-in-cheek. People were so preoccupied waiting for Tracy to show up that a woman living on a farm near the settlement of Yesler religiously put the remnants of each meal she cooked in the oven, "in the hope that Mr. Tracy will come along and feel hungry."

When Tracy was sighted in the Ballard area, the special correspondent continued in the same vein, a reporter dashed into the office of the *Post-Intelligencer* puffing and blowing like an excited porpoise.

"By George," he shouted to the city editor, "I've got a hell of a story for you!"

"What is it?"

"I shot and nearly killed Harry Tracy!"

"Shot him! Nearly killed him, you say?"

"You bet! At least, I think I wounded him. Do you want me to write a story about it?"

"Of course—if it's true."

"Well, what happened was I saw this suspicious-looking fellow behind a stump and told him to come out. He wouldn't, so I let fly. I shot at him five times. I'm sure I hit him the last time, because the son-of-a-gun doubled up and groaned."

"Where did you hit him?"

"I'm not sure. But I know I winged him because he ran out from behind the stump and disappeared into the brush." Dashing to his desk, the reporter called back over his shoulder. "I'll write the story and you can run it under my by-line in an extra. It'll go at least two columns."

Shortly thereafter, a very angry man wearing a deputy sheriff's badge burst into the city editor's office and demanded, "Have you got a damn fool reporter who's running around with a gun shooting at people?"

"Yes, I believe I do have."

"I'm Deputy Sheriff Bunce, in charge of the Tracy detail in Ballard. I was on guard this afternoon, waiting behind a stump in case Tracy came along. Then this idiot reporter came along and started shooting at me. He fired at least fourteen shots, each one missing me by a sixteenth of an inch. Now if you're going to let your reporters take target practice in Ballard, I wish you'd ask them to make sure there's no deputy sheriffs behind the stumps."

In another incident, a reporter for the Seattle *Star* was peacefully riding his bicycle along a quiet street in Renton when a man suddenly stepped out from behind a tree and began shooting at him.

"Hey!" the reporter yelled. "What are you shooting at me for?"

"I'll shoot at anyone who doesn't stop when I tell him to."

"You never told me to stop."

"Maybe I didn't. But you ought to have known enough to stop without my telling you."

Swearing that the next time he came this way he would wear a bullet-proof coat, the reporter rode back to town. "Almost every road leading through the districts over which Tracy has passed is now deserted," J.J.M. wrote. "Not because people fear the outlaw, for they are beginning to regard him with that undying affection they lavish on the Totem Pole, Elliott Bay, and anything else that bears the stamp of Seattle. It is the deputies and the reporters they fear, and with reason, for the deputies and the reporters are armed to the teeth, and their name is several times legion."

Concluding the column of Tracy tid-bits, J.J.M. revealed the exciting news that a talented local playwright, W.M. Russell, had just finished a melodrama titled "Tracy and Merrill," which would star the well-known actor, R.E. French, along with a cast that would include several actual participants in recent stirring events—playing themselves.

Planning to attend the premiere performance at the Third Avenue Theater opening night, J.J.M. promised to give his readers "as much of an idea of the drama as mere cold type can convey."

Readers were advised to await the review with bated breath . . .

TRACY IN DRAMA

Play Full of Trash That Some Seattle Folk Go to See.

IT TEACHES A LESSON ALL RIGHT

SEATTLE, July 25 —(Staff Correspondence.) Could H. Tracy, Esq., outlaw, bandit, murderer and all around bad man, but see the characterization of him which now is entertaining such of the Seattle populace as seek recreation at the Third Avenue Theater, all his glories, triumphs, spoils and other accomplishments would shrink to a very small measure, compared to the satisfaction he would derive from the performance. Tracy is more than a hero of the stage. He is a gentleman, a scholar, a tragedian, a flower of chivalry, a humorist and a philosopher. Let the average Seattle small boy witness that play and he will exchange his birthright for a .30-.30, kill his father and mother to effect his escape, and journey forth on the road, shooting down officers like chipmunks, asking fair maidens to dance and capturing whole regiments of Swedes for body-servants.

Tracy in the wild woods or the penitentiary is an uncouth thing, speaking the burglar dialect, abusing people, threatening them, bragging of his murders and promising to butcher all who attempt to interfere with his unlawful liberty. He occasionally is civil to women, in order to see his civility "played up" in the papers, which he reads regularly, but he is not the kind of gentleman one would choose for a bosom friend if one were particular.

The Mr. Tracy of the Stage.

Tracy on the stage, as interpreted by Frank Readick, is a fine-haired, chivalrous, deep-voiced and large-hearted nobleman, with a little of the Lincoln J. Carter manner, but enough of the quality that is calculated to excite the admiration of a small boy to make him exceedingly dangerous as an example. So far no evil has resulted from the play, but it has only been running a little while, and the youth of Seattle, unlike their elders of the same city, require a day or two to decide upon an important course of action.

Manager Russell has surrounded Tracy with an elaborate setting. He announces in the fearful and wonderful quarter-sheet which he has devised to advertise the play that there are 100 people on the stage, and he keeps his promise by one-half pretty well. Richard E. French, the favorite comedian, tragedian, leading man, character man and juvenile, is the Sheriff of the cast, which includes some 40 people. M.J. Hooley, who has been seen in Portland with various dramatic organizations, supplies the comedy, playing Anderson, the Swede whom Tracy kidnaped, and Samuel Halpin, who was Ralph Stuart's stage manager, plays one of the convict's pals. For a number of the others Russell has gone direct to Nature and come back smiling with the real thing. For example, the part of Charles Gerard, which is stage dialect for Gerrells, is played by the self-same Charles Gerrells who hotfooted in from Renton one day about two or three weeks ago with the news that Tracy was spending a quiet day with the Gerrells family. One of the young ladies on the stage is also one of the original people with whom Tracy talked, and she looks it.

The authors of the play disavow at the beginning of the programme any claim to literary merit for the child of their several fancies. This seems unfortunate, for the assertion of such a claim would prove them gentlemen of nerve which would make Tracy's grit look like arrant cowardice. They have taken some of the scenes in which Tracy participated, and some which they imagined, and woven them into a story which is copiously punctuated with the reports of firearms, and through which the groans of the dying play a ragtime obligato.

First Act Opens at Salem.

The first act opens at Salem, with the guards at the penitentiary yard engaged in a premonition fest. They all know that something is going to happen, and they are inclined to believe that Tracy and Merrill are mixed up in it, but they take no precautions to watch these worthies, who presently come in, extract two rifles from their toolboxes and begin to shoot up everybody in sight. Amid the wails of the wounded and the vows of vengeance of the one survivor the curtain goes down.

Tracy next appears alone. He shows up in the second act at the cabin of Captain Clark, near Olympia, and holds up all hands. Again, he turns up loose at Seattle, unlimbers his gun on everybody on the stage, kills them all with the exception of the assistant property-man, and retreats to the wings in triumph.

The scene is now transferred across Puget Sound, where the hero invades the Johnson cabin, annexes Anderson to his staff, and, assuring Mrs. Johnson that no harm shall come to her, bows himself out. It is at Renton that he next bursts upon the view of the now thoroughly sympathetic audience. He meets the ladies in front of the Gerrells residence, assures them repeatedly that no harm shall come to them, takes a shot or two at such reckless supernumeraries as happen to cross the stage, and departs. The remaining scenes are destitute of bloodshed up to the last, when Tracy, after a grand, heroic battle, gives up his life for his freedom.

The managers of the play announce that it teaches a lesson. It does. Seattle will get the benefit of it as soon as the youngsters have had time to lay in a stock of firearms. J.J.M.

Avid drama-lover that he was, Harry Tracy himself probably would have been in the audience if invited to attend the production. An announcement of his presence would have filled the theatre for weeks to come if, during the curtain calls, he had stepped up in the stage and taken a bow . . .

Discoverers of Merrill's body

MRS. MARY WAGGONER AND HER SON, GEORGE, OF NAPAVINE, WASH.

Oregonian clipping

A critical review

OFF THE STAGE FOR A BRIEF SEASON ONLY

BAD MAN TRACY—"Ladies and gentlemen, as the posse in the cast is behind in its lines, there will be a short intermission."

Oregonian

UT

in

[AD

Tries
ho

OUT

he im-
itsiders
· Cam-
· a law
Rolling
id four-
om the
ll make

rescue

any de-
he work
nt into
horrible
· trans-
nbulance
of the
ng from
n, bend-
carried
ground
to take

he after-
he inner-
life yet
the left
nable to
te even
one that
s of roof
through
ve men
t, young
r, Philip
· Martins

ng

hey were
hich em-
t rushed
The man
nd tried
reecuers.
red back
the cars.
found in
· quick-

rrs came
ting am-
ere lifted.
half car-
strapping
he rea·h-
pent sev-

As the

TRACY SEEKS SAFETY
IN GINTER SWAMP

DRIVEN THERE BY BLOODHOUNDS

Exciting Chase Led Over Trail of Desperado by Sheriff Cudihee, Following Midnight Encounters Near Covington

CENTER OF ACTION AT RAVENSDALE

HARRY TRACY plunged into the thick undergrowth of Ginter swamp, southeast of Black Diamond, early yesterday afternoon, ending the day's pursuit by the bloodhounds and sheriff's posses. In this morass he is believed to have spent all the late part of the afternoon and early evening. When darkness fell, it is thought he cautiously left the thickets about the edge of the swamps and made for Palmer, the district it is generally accepted he is determined to reach. These suggested plans of the outlaw, deduced from his talk since leaving the Gerrells home at Renton Tuesday and his actions in Thursday night's battle are being counted on in maneuvers for the desperado's capture by Sheriff Cudihee.

Sheriff Cudihee has changed his headquarters to Ravensdale and from that point is personally directing the movements of his deputies. Last night he placed a large number of them in advantageous positions calculated to cover the possible retreat or advance of the fugitive. The sheriff has reduced his force of men to only those who have had actual experience in fighting and are implicitly trusted. In placing the guards and planning to hem in the convict, the sheriff has employed considerable secrecy. This has been made necessary because of the outlaw's accomplices.

In summing up the chase since first Tracy landed on Meadow point in King county, last night Sheriff Cudihee expressed the opinion that the outlaw is now in the most dangerous position he has yet occupied. Cudihee will not give up the fight so long as Tracy remains uncaptured in Western Washington. He is known to be completely exhausted and is suffering keenly from the hardships of the past few days' travel. Besides this, the theory is advanced that he may be wounded as the result of Thursday night's collision with the Bunces. All these facts point to possible sensational developments today,

By a Staff Correspondent.
BLACK DIAMOND, July 11.—With the deep baying of the bloodhounds ringing in his ears, Harry Tracy, the outlaw convict, fled into Ginter swamp, between here and Ravensdale, this afternoon and succeeded in escaping, throwing the pursuing posse for the time off his track. It is stated on the best of authority that Sheriff Cudihee has learned that Tracy is heading for Palmer Junction in the hopes of joining Merrill, his partner in crime, and of obtaining assistance in making his

close range from the shotguns of J. A. and Fred Bunce, whom he passed at 12:10 o'clock this morning in a deep railroad cut a half mile west of Covington station. After escaping this fire and by a clever ruse deceiving a deputy stationed 200 yards further up the track, Tracy again vanised for the time and tonight his pursuers are at sea as to his exact whereabouts.

The chase has now resolved itself into a grim and dogged determination on the part of the sheriff and his deputies to stay with the chase to the bitter end, notwithstanding the demoralizing report cir-

through where the shooting took place some one in the bushes called to the crew to stop, but the conductor did not heed and came through to Covington, where he related the circumstance. As no deputies were in the locality at the time, it was thought that Tracy, maddened by wound, had uttered the cry. As soon as possible after receiving the report Sheriff Cudihee, who was at Auburn, assembled the guards in that vicinity, and with Guard Carson and the bloodhounds arrived at Covington at 8 o'clock this morning. The dogs took up the scent where the battle occurred and followed

CHAPTER ELEVEN
WHERE DID TRACY GO?

For the next week or so, Tracy-sightings were few and far between. Since shots had recently been exchanged between deputies and a man thought to be Tracy, Sheriff Cudihee had reason to believe that he had been wounded and now was holed up somewhere nursing what the sheriff hoped would become a fatal case of blood-poisoning.

In one confirmed encounter, Tracy had visited the cabin of an elderly French-Canadian couple named Portaut, who lived in the woods near Auburn. So badly wounded he could barely walk and so sick he could barely eat, he showed up at their home at 4:30 one afternoon, stayed only an hour or so, then vanished into the thick cover along Green River. Other than giving them the fright of their lives, he did them no harm. When interviewed by a reporter the day after his visit, the Portauts were still trembling.

Tracy looked like a physical wreck, they said. His left leg was practically useless, his back was bloody with a deep laceration, and every movement caused him pain.

"I got wounded in the back just above the left hip," Tracy told them. "I was hit with a charge of buckshot last night, and the wound is still bleeding."

When Mrs. Portaut set a simple meal of bread, butter, milk, and a piece of pie in front of him, a couple of bites of pie and half a glass of milk were all he could get down. While he was eating, a buggy carrying Deputy Sheriff Fred Berner and three possemen came along the road in front of the house. Jumping to his feet and grabbing his rifle, Tracy moved from the kitchen into the bedroom, warning the couple:

"You have nothing to gain by giving me away."

Frightened as they were, the last thing his hosts were likely to do was jeopardize their lives by betraying him. While in the house, he treated Mrs. Portaut with his usual deference, at one time even stifling "a profane epithet" because of the lady's presence.

"He did not look like a criminal," Mrs. Portaut told the reporter. "He treated us very nicely, and it is hard to believe that he has such a black record."

On one of those rare occasions when Sheriff Cudihee—who lately was becoming very shy with the press—consented to being interviewed, he said that Tracy probably would try to cross the Cascades and get into eastern Washington, when and if he recovered enough from his wound to travel.

"Tracy can only pass over the mountain range at two points," Cudihee told a *P-I* reporter. "One way is to follow up the Green River valley and cross the Stampede Pass where the Northern Pacific goes through. The other is to take the partly completed state road, built in 1896, that leads from the White River across the Naches Pass to the headwaters of the Yakima. The latter is a difficult route and uninhabited the entire distance." (So difficult that the highway across this route was not completed until sixty years later.)

"It is almost beyond reason that he can ever cross the mountains, but if he does he will stand small chance in open prairies where speed is the only assurance of safety."

What Sheriff Cudihee was *not* telling the press, to its great exasperation, were the details of a scheme he had been cooking up with a "stool pigeon" (yes, the term was in use in 1902) to find out where Tracy was hiding and capture or kill him *sans* media coverage. What kind of an event would closing in for the kill be without newsmen present? the reporters were asking indignantly. Nevertheless, Sheriff Cudihee seemed determined to do it his way. A reporter wrote:

That Sheriff Cudihee had unlimited faith in the information furnished him, is shown by the elaborate plans which were laid. On Tuesday night Cudihee appeared at Covington with the Whatcom stool pigeon, and on Wednesday evening disappeared for several hours in company with the latter. It is understood that the sheriff attempted to prevail upon his informant to lead a posse of selected men to the cabin where he claimed Tracy was lying wounded and unable to move without assistance. To this Tracy's betrayer demurred at the last moment, claiming that he would as soon be shot dead on the spot as pilot the posse and subject himself to the fire of Tracy and his confederates, spurred on by the knowledge that he had revealed their retreat to officers of the law.

Thrown upon his own resources, Cudihee assembled a posse of twelve men under the guidance of Jack Fraser, left Covington Wednesday night, and headed for the isolated cabin on the shores of Lake Sawyer, where the stool pigeon had told him Tracy was hiding.

Twice the party got lost, but finally emerged a stone's throw from the cabin. It was now daylight. After a hurried conversation, the sheriff determined to make a quick descent upon the place and beard the lion in his den. A reporter wrote:

At a given signal, all hands made a grand rush for the cabin, bursting inside, only to find that if Harry Tracy had ever been its occupant, he had flown. A smoldering fire gave mute evidence that some human being had recently frequented the premises, and a linen rag, upon which two members of the posse claim to have detected faint blood stains, was found inside the cabin.

Sheriff Cudihee had again failed to realize his hopes, the reporter gloated, implying that it served him right for not inviting the press to participate in the adventure. Which left the paramount question still up in the air:

"Where is convict Harry Tracy?"

Rubbing salt into the lacerations to Sheriff Cudihee's wounded pride, the reporter spitefully raised the possibility that Cudihee had been set up by the so-called "stool pigeon," who had encouraged him to assemble a posse and raid an empty cabin in one area of the Green River wilderness so that the way would be cleared for Tracy to escape via another route, which by this ruse would be left unguarded.

But as Sheriff Cudihee and all the other law officers who had pursued Harry Tracy for the past six weeks knew very well, Tracy required no help when it came to avoiding efforts to contain him. When he wanted to travel in a certain direction at a certain time, he did so—and no one could stop him.

Right now, he appeared to want to cross the mountains. In all likelihood, that was exactly what he would do—unless, of course, he did the unexpected, as he often did . . .

Even though David Merrill was dead and buried under four feet of earth in the prison yard at Salem, he was still the subject of controversy. Since the reward for the capture and return of the two escaped convicts "dead or alive" had risen to $6,000, the question now was: how much were the remains of Merrill worth? Did the mere discovery of those remains by Mrs. Mary Waggoner and her son George constitute "capture?" Further complicating the issue was the fact that the dead convict's brother, Ben Merrill, claimed he would have given the remains a proper Christian burial if they had not been rudely snatched away from him by the sovereign state of Oregon.

All of this was aired in the columns of the *Oregonian* in the form of an open letter from prison Superintendent Lee to Ben Merrill, dated July 22:

> *Dear Sir: It will no doubt surprise you to be addressed by one who never met you, and especially through the press, but the message is an important one and much of it interests the public as well as yourself. My attention has been called to the following item in a recent issue of the* Evening Telegram *of Portland:*
>
> *"Though only a workingman on small wages, Ben H. Merrill offered more money for his brother's body than*

the State of Oregon. He said he would pay whatever I asked," said Mrs. Mary Waggoner, who discovered the remains, "if I would help him to keep the matter quiet and let him bury the body. He intended to pay it out of his wages in installments."

It was with surprise, Mr. Merrill, that I read the above. It was new to me. Was it possible that I had been a party, though unwittingly, to a transaction that deprived you of the sacred privilege of giving a decent and honorable burial to a brother? I had been informed before beginning negotiations with the party above quoted that you favored interment in the prison cemetery.

I have never refused the request of relatives for the body of a deceased prisoner. Big-hearted Tom Benton (his predecessor) once said: "When God lays hands on a man, Tom Benton takes his hands off."

The question is: What can I do in the line of practical relief? It is this: That upon your instruction, sir, certified to by a magistrate with a seal, I will forward the remains to any railroad station in Western Washington.

Should you feel any hesitancy in so doing, from suggestions in any quarter that I wish to get some technical advantage of the claimant of the reward for the capture and return of David Merrill, dead or alive, permit me to disabuse your mind of any such thought. The State of Oregon is not dealing in technicalities, but wishes to meet its promises in their true spirit and intent.

The central thought—the philosophy—of a reward for the capture and return of a desperate fugitive is that fearless and efficient men may be compensated for the risk of life and limb they take in attempting his capture. Sometimes, in such effort, his life must be taken; hence the further condition that the reward will be good if such should be the case. Thus heroism is encouraged and rewarded and society protected. The accidental finding of a corpse is in no true sense a capture. It is

only by the most technical and ungenerous reasoning
that any such conclusion can be reached.
The only question now at issue is that of compensa-
tion for the return of the body, which the state proposes
to make. Whether the powers above me increase or
diminish the present offer, the principle remains the
same. This explanation, I trust, will be sufficient to give
you full assurance of my desire to meet your wishes and
overcome all hesitancy you may have in making the
request for David's body.
                    Respectfully yours, J.D. Lee, Supt. Oregon State
                                                      Penitentiary.

A few days later, Governor Geer held a conference with
Superintendent Lee regarding payment of the reward for the
finding and return of the body. No final conclusion could be
reached, he announced, until the identity of the remains was
established beyond a doubt.

"The state is not disposed to quibble over the matter," said
Governor Geer, "but it would place us in a very bad position if
we should pay the reward and then Merrill should later turn
up. From the reports I have heard, I am inclined to presume
that the body returned is indeed Merrill's, but since I have not
yet had an opportunity to talk to Warden Janes, I will take no
immediate action. There is no need to hurry the matter."

As to whether a substantial portion of the reward—say, half
of the total of $6,000 offered for the two men—would be paid to
Mrs. Waggoner, the statement made by Governor Geer was a
clear warning that she should make no expensive purchases in
the near future. It seemed to him, Governor Geer said, that
"capture and return" did not mean stumbling upon a corpse
while picking berries in the woods.

"It is worth something to the state to have the body of the
escaped convict returned, and the person furnishing the evidence of the death of Merrill should be paid liberally."

Promising to consider all phases of the question and try to do
justice to all concerned, the governor further dampened Mrs.
Waggoner's hopes for a generous reward by saying that whatever amount her grant might be reduced would be added to the

reward being offered for the "capture and return" of Harry Tracy, "dead or alive."

Meantime, newspaper readers in Washington, Oregon, and wherever the syndicated stories were being fed to Tracy aficionados all over the United States were growing tired of reading about buried remains and demanding that the reporters get back to the chase, answering the burning question:

Where is Harry Tracy?

The answer seemed to be: "All over the place."

A special dispatch to the Seattle *Post-Intelligencer* July 23 from Roslyn, Washington, stated that a man reported to be Harry Tracy spent Sunday and Monday at Camp Creek, twenty miles from Roslyn, in Kittitas County, east of the Cascades, having taken a freight train across the mountains to that place. After being fed and having a deep wound on his left forearm dressed by friendly coal miners, he and several heavily armed companions with whom he was traveling went fishing and caught eighteen trout.

"He said he is on his way East to see his mother," the news item stated, "after which he will give himself up."

On that same day and in the same column, another news item announced that Tracy had appeared in a logging camp near Tacoma, again being fed by friendly people, who asked him why he did not hop on a freight train and seek freedom east of the mountains.

"I have some business to settle with Merrill's brother," he answered grimly. "I understand that the brother wants to see me."

Whether the brother was Ben seeking a loan in order to pay for re-burying his brother's remains was a question neither asked nor answered. The nameless logger quoted in the news item did say that Tracy was not wounded and looked fresh and rested.

"He was wearing a derby hat. He had a slouch hat in his pocket. He still had his Winchester, two revolvers, and a good supply of ammunition."

In the adjoining column of the same paper, a story from Salem, Oregon put a question mark after a headline reading:

IS TRACY AGAIN NEAR SALEM?

A man answering Tracy's description was one of three men seen near here on bicycles at seven o'clock last evening. All were heavily armed. The prison authorities were at once notified, and Superintendent J.D. Lee immediately took precautions to prevent any entrance into the prison by the outlaws by placing extra guards on the walls and sending out a full force to surround the prison yard.

In case Harry Tracy was indulging in one of his favorite pursuits, reading the newspapers, a story under the above headline dated July 23 gave him fair warning that his visit was anticipated.

The Oregon Penitentiary is surrounded tonight by armed guards, watching for the appearance of Desperado Tracy. While it is not believed that the men seen in the vicinity are Tracy and confederates, the prison officials are proceeding on the theory that the report received may be correct. There is practically a dead-line extending around the prison at the distance of a rifle shot, and prison guards tonight have telephoned the Sheriff not to approach the Penitentiary unless called for, as he might be shot by the sentinels. Any man who goes near the Penitentiary at night does so at his peril.

Thanks to the precautions taken by Superintendent Lee, nobody—including Harry Tracy—risked getting shot by trying to break *into* the prison that night . . .

The rumor that Tracy had crossed the Cascades and was now active in the eastern part of the state proved to be true. On a sunny morning in late July, the outlaw came into a sheep camp on Wilson Creek, twenty-five miles north of Ellensburg. The owner of the band of sheep, W.B. Dunsworth, was absent at the time, having gone into Ellensburg for a load of provisions, but the herder, who was not named in the news report, later told his employer what happened.

The gaunt, weary, fierce-looking man who came into camp a little after nine o'clock identified himself as Harry Tracy, the herder said, and stayed for six hours. He made no threats, but helped himself to food and clothes. After eating two hearty meals, he divided the remaining provisions into equal portions, leaving half of them with the herder and taking the other half with him.

Practically barefoot and poorly dressed, he took a good pair of shoes and a nearly new pair of overalls. When he saw the herder's .30-.30 Winchester rifle, his eyes lighted up, and he exclaimed, "I must have your rifle, too."

"Please don't take it, Mr. Tracy," the sheepherder begged. "It's the only gun I've got to protect the sheep from coyotes and wolves."

"I need protection, too. I've got to have it, friend."

"You've already got a rifle, haven't you?"

"Yeah. But it's not much good."

"Will it shoot?"

"Oh, sure, but it's been used hard and ain't in very good order."

"Leave it with me, then. At least, I'll have some kind of a gun."

After a moment's hesitation, Tracy shook his head. "Can't do it, old timer. I promised to pay the man who smuggled it into the penitentiary for me $5,000 as soon as I could raise the money. The officers know the registration number on the rifle. If they found it, they could trace it back to him and learn who he is. I'll never give him away."

"What will you do with it?"

"Throw it in the Columbia River, maybe. Or smash it up against a rockpile so that it can't be identified. But I ain't going to let it out of my hands."

When ready to go, Tracy made out an inventory of what he was taking, the herder said, including two horses, and said he would send back payment when he got settled. He then rode off on one of the horses, a bald-faced sorrel, saying he would turn

the horses loose at the river, which he later did, for both animals returned to the camp a few days later.

Learning that owner Dunsworth would be on his way back
from Ellensburg presently, Tracy told the herder that he
planned to hold him up, but missed him, and did not do so. In
all, the rifle and provisions Tracy took from the sheep camp
were worth around forty dollars, Dunsworth later told a
reporter for the *Spokesman-Review.*

"Tracy wants to hold up a bank or rob an express car,"
Dunsworth said. "He says he's promised to give five thousand
dollars to the parties who helped him escape from the Oregon
Penitentiary. He says he's making his way to the 'Hole-in-the-
Wall' hideout where a lot of outlaws go. When there, he says,
he'll be a 'thief among thieves,' and will be safe."

At ten o'clock, next morning, Wenatchee City Councilman
W.A. Sanders, who was spending the day at a farm owned by
his son-in-law, Sam MacEldowney, was approached by a man
who had just ridden up on horseback. Busy packing fruit in a
shed on the farm, Sanders noted that the man had the appearance of a sheepherder, many of whom passed that way, so, without pausing in his work, merely nodded and said pleasantly,
"Good day."

"I am Harry Tracy, the convict," the man said, trying to
divert Sanders' attention from packing fruit to himself.

Thinking the stranger was joking, Sanders smiled and said,
"Help yourself to an apricot, Mr. Tracy."

"I can see you don't believe me," the stranger said, drawing
a revolver and placing its muzzle a few inches from the busy
fruit packer's nose, "but perhaps this will help you to realize
that I am telling the truth."

It did.

"Very well, Mr. Tracy," Sanders said politely. "What do you
want?"

"Well, for the present, I want you to keep quiet. I don't want
any disturbances. I want to rest."

For the next two hours, Sanders later told reporters, relatives, and friends, he packed fruit so quietly one apricot could
not be heard brushing its fuzz against another. While Tracy

lounged on a pile of gunny sacks in the coolness of the shed's interior and his horses dozed on their feet in the shade outside, Sanders studied the outlaw covertly, worrying over what he might do. Though he had said he wanted to rest, he did not doze or close his eyes, keeping up a continual nervous chatter about the weather, the heat, and the fruit crop, without giving away any information about where he had recently been or where he intended to go. Jumpy though he was, he seemed to be in good spirits and showed no signs of being wounded.

At noon, Sam MacEldowney, W.A. Sanders' son-in-law, came to the shed and said it was time for dinner. Seeing a stranger present, he invited him to stay and eat with the family.

"Mr. MacEldowney," said Sanders, "this is Mr. Tracy."

Not catching the name, MacEldowney acknowledged the introduction and turned to go.

"Stop, Sam," Tracy said. "I see you don't remember me."

MacEldowney, who had formerly lived in Portland and had known Tracy before his conviction, whirled around and studied him more closely.

"My God!" he exclaimed. "It's Harry Tracy!"

Tracy now took charge of all proceedings, following Sanders and MacEldowney rifle in hand as the trio walked up to the house. Two farmhands were about to sit down and eat when Tracy ushered his hostages in and said:

"My friends, Mr. MacEldowney knows who I am, and that what I say goes. Do just as I say."

Getting no argument from the diners, he then directed them all to sit on one side of the table, while he seated himself on the other, so that he could watch the doors leading to the other rooms. Though everyone was nervous, the meal was eaten quietly. Thinking it would be cooler outside, he let everybody go out on the porch when the meal was over, permitting some of the family members to seek shade trees in the yard, while he and his ever-present rifle pre-empted a spot on the porch from which he could keep an eye on everybody.

"The afternoon," Sanders said later, "dragged slowly."

During the long afternoon, Tracy showed marked signs of nervousness, Sanders said, "Lying down, jumping up, pacing like a caged animal. He talked rapidly, almost hysterically at times, but with it all he avoided all reference to his past or future course."

When supper time came, he allowed Mrs. MacEldowney to prepare and serve the meal as she had done at noon. When it was over, he began to show signs of activity, ordering his horses unsaddled and looking them over critically. They were good horses, Sanders said, one a bay and the other a buckskin, but they showed signs of having been ridden far and hard. Seeing no other suitable horses in the corral to replace them, Tracy ordered the bay and the buckskin re-saddled and said that he was going to leave now, taking Sam MacEldowney along as a hostage and guide.

"At this announcement," Sanders said, "Mrs. MacEldowney, whose nerves were already strained, broke down and began crying violently. The little children joined in chorus with their mother."

This was too much for Tracy, who turned to MacEldowney in exasperation and said:

"Damn it, man, your wife will cry all night, won't she? I have a heart left yet. I won't take you along."

"We thank you for that."

"One favor deserves another, Sam. Can you get me a couple of good horses?"

"You're welcome to what I have here."

"They won't do. I want strong, fresh horses. They must be shod. What have your neighbors got?"

In view from the house in the pasture of a neighbor named Lockwood, a number of horses could be seen. "Sam," Tracy asked, "are those horses any good?"

"Yes, I think some of them are."

"Then get them for me."

Covered by Tracy's rifle, MacEldowney went into the pasture of his neighbor, who was not home, and returned with three horses, which Tracy examined carefully. Finding them in good condition and well shod, Tracy ordered them saddled and then made MacEldowney mount and ride each one in turn to show their paces. Satisfied that they would do, Tracy had a good-sized gray saddled to ride himself, while his pack-saddle was placed on a slightly smaller sorrel, which he would lead.

"Don't leave the premises for twenty-four hours," he warned his involuntary hosts, "or tell anybody I was here. If you do, I'll come back and kill you all."

Like many families Tracy had visited before, this one was so sure he meant what he said that they obeyed his ultimatum almost to the letter.

"All night we waited in suspense," Sanders said later. "This morning, seeing no signs of anyone in the vicinity, MacEldowney followed the horse tracks far enough to satisfy himself that Tracy had taken the road down to the river, and then went into town, reaching there about 2 p.m., where he notified the authorities."

Before leaving the ranch, Tracy had said he planned to cross the Columbia River at Mottler's Ferry, then ride east across Washington, Idaho, and Montana, into Wyoming, where he would join his friends in the "Hole-in-the-Wall" gang and be safe as "a thief among thieves." Though earlier he had been identified with a "Hole-in-the-Wall" gang in Utah, Butch Cassidy, the Sundance Kid, and their "Hole-in-the-Wall" gang were headquartered in Wyoming. Some geographically ignorant reporters even called unrelated places such as Jackson Hole a gang hideout. Inveterate newspaper reader that he was, Tracy probably relished contributing to the confusion.

In any event, Tracy did show up at Mottlers Ferry on the west bank of the Columbia, twelve miles from the ranch, an hour after dark. Without informing the brothers who operated the toll ferry who he was, he demanded to be taken across the river immediately. Telling him that the rapids-filled, swollen river was too dangerous to cross at night, they forced him to wait until dawn next morning. Noting that he was a hard-looking character who did not sleep at all that night, loosening the cinches but not unsaddling his horses, staying near them and pacing up and down all night, the Mottler brothers were not too surprised when, after they had ferried him and his horses across the river in the dawn's gray light, he told them he was broke and could not pay them, even if he felt like doing so, which he did not.

Glad to be rid of him, they let him go. When told later who he was, they were not surprised.

In contrast to the green, well-watered, tree-and-bush covered country west of the Cascade, this land east of the mountains was open, dusty, dry, desert country, where a man on a horse could be seen miles away. No doubt Sheriff Edward Cudihee, who was still in pursuit of Tracy, felt much more at home here than he did in King County, for the wide reaches of space across which he and local Sheriff De Bolt of Douglas County were trailing their man reminded him of the high mesa and mountain terrain west of the Rockies near Leadville, Colorado, where he had made his reputation of always getting his man.

Certainly, if Cudihee had faults, lack of perseverance was not one of them. Believing that Tracy was somewhere on the fifty miles of road between Connewai Creek and Davenport, Washington, the two officers left Almira at three o'clock in the morning and traveled until eleven, when they learned from a man they encountered that a rider leading a packhorse had passed that way the evening before.

Local people, who knew the country between Wenatchee and Spokane, expressed disbelief that Tracy could cross Grand Coulee without guidance from someone familiar with the area, for the 800-foot deep, five-mile-wide, fifty-mile-long, sheer-walled gash in the volcanic terrain was impassable except in a place or two. But with or without assistance, Tracy kept going.

The man was seen by several people, who said that his pack horse was dragging a rope. The rope mark was tracked in the dusty road for about twelve miles to the home of John Sterett, on Connewai Creek. There it was learned that the man with the horses had inquired the way to Davenport about ten o'clock Saturday night.

Compared to following bloodhounds afoot through wet ferns and tall trees, this was tracking as it should be done, Sheriff Cudihee must have thought, in the tradition of Western novels written by Zane Grey, and, a few years later, by William McCleod Raine. As a matter of fact, Raine, then a young newspaper reporter in Denver, happened to be visiting relatives in the Seattle area during the time Tracy was on the loose. Many years afterward, with his fame as a Western novelist well established, Raine wrote that he had interviewed a member of the crew of the gasoline launch that had transported Tracy from Olympia to Seattle, adding:

> *Later, in the capacity of a newspaper correspondent, I saw a good deal of the men who had charge of the capture of the outlaw and was at one time with the posse (entirely as a pacifist) which operated near Bothell.*

Showing good sense then as he later would in his novels, William McCleod Raine might have written a scene in which a pair of outlaws agreed to fight a duel by standing back-to-back, taking ten paces each, then turning to fire. But his fictional code of honor would not have allowed either one of them to cheat.

Learning from rope marks in the dust that Tracy had backtracked from the Sterett house and turned north, the two sheriffs and a reporter from the *Spokesman-Review*, who was riding with them, turned north, too, lost the trail for a time in barren, rocky terrain, then picked it up again after three-quarters of a mile. At two o'clock in the afternoon, having been in the saddle for eleven straight hours, the two officers lost the reporter, too.

Using the lame excuse that he had to ride into the ten-mile-distant railroad town of Krupp, Washington on the Great Northern to file his story on the chase, the reporter rode stiffly away. Since the story he filed revealed no sensational new developments, uncharitable readers may have suspected that the reporter was suffering from rump-lameness after his long day in the saddle rather than from being imbued with journalistic enterprise. In any case, this was the news item he filed:

> *Since then, the officers have not been seen; but if nothing has occurred to send them off on a new trail, they are on their long journey to Davenport. They are cut off from telegraphic communication, and will probably have to camp out on the road tonight.*

The supposition is that Tracy is traveling by night, and they hope either to intercept him on the road or swoop down on his camp early in the morning.

Though the word "trapped" at first glance does not seem suitable to describe Tracy's predicament in the wide-open, big-country terrain of northeast Washington, it fitted his present situation far better than when he had been at large in the Seattle area. In the thick cover west of the Cascades, a fugitive could disappear simply by stepping into the undergrowth ten feet off a well-traveled trail or road. On the mesas, plains, and scablands of eastern Washington, a fleeing man or his dusty trail could be seen as far as the eye could reach, so he was easy to keep track of. A Spokane news item stated:

The pursuers of Tracy are proceeding on the theory that he is somewhere in the southeastern portion of Lincoln County. Sheriffs Cudihee and De Bolt arrived at Rearden, fifteen miles east of Davenport, at an early hour this morning, having traveled all night. Sheriff Doust, of Spokane County, and a posse are guarding the Sprague country. Sheriff Gardner, of Lincoln, is still covering the northern end of the county.

Though a map of the area across which Tracy was known to be moving showed the distance between Wenatchee on the west and Spokane on the east to be 175 miles, while from Moses Lake on the south to Chelan on the north it measured ninety miles, the search area was pinpointed, in a sense, by the fact that the distance a man could travel on horseback during a given period of time was known, as was the fact that, even if his riding were done at night when he himself could not be seen, there was no way he could travel without leaving a trail. Furthermore, no matter how fast he rode, the network of tele-graph and telephone lines covering the country could warn law officers and posse members of his movements much faster.

Apparently reading the newspapers again, Tracy learned that Sheriff Cudihee was still on his trail. He used the August 5 *Spokesman-Review* to send a message.

A WARNING TO CUDIHEE.

Tracy Says He Will Shoot Sheriff if He Does Not Let Him Alone.

To Whom It May Concern, Tracy scrawled in a note pinned to the well of farmer C.V. Drazon, where Tracy had stopped during the hours just before dawn to water his horses.

Tell Mr. Cudihee to take a tumble and let me alone, or I will fix him plenty. I will be on my way to Wyoming. If your horses was any good would swap with you. Thanks for a cool drink.

HARRY TRACY.

Either in no hurry or uncertain how to evade the net that was closing in around him, Tracy took five days to travel a distance a man on horseback ordinarily could traverse in one. Going back to his old tactic of moving in and taking over a house in a remote location, he appeared at the home of L.B. Eddy, a rancher who lived on Lake Creek, about three and one-half miles south of the small settlement of Fellows, Washington, which was ten miles distant from the larger town of Creston, Washington, fifty-four miles west of Spokane. Though this was as remote an area as any to be found in the region, it was one in which the presence of a famous killer outlaw who had led hundreds of law officers and possemen on a merry chase for almost two months could not be overlooked.

Unless a miracle happened, the final scene of the drama appeared to be at hand. But Harry Tracy on many previous occasions had proved himself to be a miracle-worker . . .

Meantime, in Salem, Oregon, Governor Geer advised Mrs. Mary Waggoner that in order to proceed regularly in demanding payment of the reward for the capture and return of convict David Merrill she must file a formal claim with the Secretary of State, who, as auditor, would pass upon the legality of the claim.

The *Oregonian* reported that,

*No such claim has been filed, but Mrs. Waggoner has
asked Superintendent Lee to pay the reward, thinking
that he has the authority to do so. Secretary of State
Dunbar declines to say what view he takes of the matter, and will not pass upon Mrs. Waggoner's right to the
$1,500 until the claim comes before him in proper form.*

When, why, and how the reward Frank Scott had thought
would be $6,000 had been reduced to $1,500, the news story did
not say. Nor was the name of Frank Scott mentioned.

In Portland, a woman named Mrs. Rottner, 207 Market, who
now lived in the very house in which David Merrill had been
arrested, told a reporter:

*I remember I had a Harry Tracy as one of my board-
ers at the First Street house about the year 1890. I cannot say if he is the Harry Tracy who was with Merrill.
If he is, he owes me fifty dollars—and I wish he would
pay up before he gets killed.*

In Chehalis, Washington, close to the site where the duel had
been fought and David Merrill's remains found, freedom of
expression suffered a serious blow when a news item
announced:

*The Tracy and Merrill show did not perform last
night in Chehalis as advertised. The City Council
refused a license for the performance.*

On August 2, the *Oregonian* printed a brief follow-up news
item stating that Frank Ingram, the prisoner at the Salem
Penitentiary who had tried to stop Tracy and Merrill from
escaping and had been shot for his effort, had been released
from the hospital after a seven-week stay.

*His left leg was amputated above the knee and he
walks on crutches. As he is unable to make a living at
present by working, he is raffling off a splendid set of
steel hearth utensils made by him while confined in the
Penitentiary. When his means will permit, he will*

purchase an artificial limb and engage in some useful occupation.

During his ten years incarceration, Ingram learned the blacksmith's trade, but the loss of his limb will probably prevent him from continuing in that work. Ingram grappled with Merrill while the latter was in the act of firing at a prison guard, and the bullet passed through his knee. His heroic act led to his pardon by the Governor and won him the sympathy of the people. He is receiving temporary aid here from people who are charitably disposed.

The same issue of the paper contained a box announcing a coming attraction which was probably of more interest to the reader.

WHY THE PURSUIT
OF TRACY FAILED

Tomorrow's Oregonian *will contain an article by Walter Lyon, private secretary of Governor Geer, reviewing the pursuit of Tracy, and showing why it failed. It is well worth reading. In connection with this article, there is published briefly Tracy's career in the "Hole-in-the-Wall," a wild district in Utah, which he is now trying to reach. His crimes and his desperate character were well known to the officers of the Oregon Penitentiary, who were advised to keep him chained like a wild beast.*

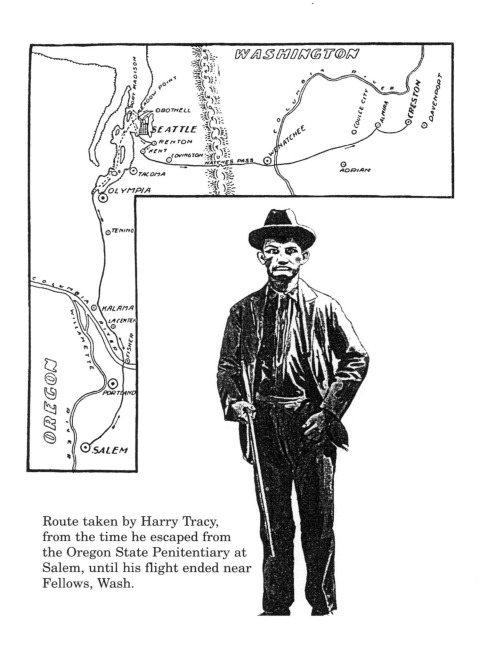

Route taken by Harry Tracy,
from the time he escaped from
the Oregon State Penitentiary at
Salem, until his flight ended near
Fellows, Wash.

CHAPTER TWELVE

WHY THE PURSUIT FAILED

A s promised to readers of the *Oregonian* the day before, the issue published Sunday, August 3, 1902, contained a long, well-reasoned, impeccably logical article by Walter Lyon, Secretary to Oregon Governor Geer, stating the reasons why Harry Tracy had not been caught. Safely protected within the walls of his capitol building office 400 miles from the sheep camp where Tracy was last reported seen, Secretary Lyon wrote:

> *Let us take this opportunity to learn something about the character of Harry Tracy as a fugitive, observing some of the things regarding the pursuit of him, following the chase for the fifty-five days he has led or dodged the posses through Oregon and Washington.*
>
> *The public is already familiar with that chapter in the eventful saga of Tracy's escape beginning at 7 o'clock on the morning of June 9 when he and Merrill, with their murderous rifles, shot and killed three of the penitentiary guards, wounded a convict, and scaled the prison walls, with Tracy continuing his flight north until having killed, first his pal, then three officers of the State of Washington. After wounding a fourth, he then vanished in the forest in the vicinity of Seattle, King County, on the 23rd day of July. During this time, Tracy baffled Sheriffs, eluded a pack of bloodhounds,*

derided deputies, mocked the armed militia, and made a sorry spectacle of professional manhunters, maintaining his liberty in defiance of all the military authorites, equipped with Winchesters, Springfields, Jaegers, Marlins, Savages and other weapons, that were on his trail.

Many times during the chase, Tracy was within gunshot range of his pursuers, yet his hiding places proved as unknowable to the men trying to find him as any the wilds of South Africa afforded.

Lost Opportunities.

That he played in luck, all familiar with his escapades will agree. That he was not captured or killed was not all his fault. He might have been shot while climbing the penitentiary walls. There was a possibility of closing down his existence at Gervais. Charley Dunlap could have sent a Savage bullet through him near La Center by merely pulling the trigger. Bert Biesecker and Luther Davidson could have shot him at Salmon Creek. It was quite possible for the four men who conveyed him from Olympia to Meadow Point to have overpowered him and taken his guns. In Bothell at the Van Horn house he might have been killed, and near there Deputy Crow might have shot him in the railroad cut near Covington.

He should have been captured at the Gerrells residence near Renton, where he let down his guard. The nester, Johnson, of Kent, might have effected a capture at his home, instead of supplying Tracy with firearms. Quick action on the part of the posse there would at least have resulted in a battle. But Tracy still lives to convince himself that he is not a victim of what might have been. Favored by too many moments of hesitation or blunder of the possemen, supplemented by Tracy's ability to take advantage of situations as they arose, he continues to win out.

How Tracy Chose Paths.

All the way from Salem to Puget Sound there is a continuous stretch of timber, and in this wooded way

Tracy steadfastly kept his course, making an occasional foray out into open country and the settlements where food is plentiful. This timber belt is marked with many canyons and thick growths of salal brush, fern, vine maple, and other forest shrubbery, interspersed with fallen trees and covered with heavy foliage which defies the penetration of the bloodhounds, inviting only owls and animals of the forest. County roads, however, occasionally cross the thickets, and some sections are checkered by log and skid roads, cowpaths, and narrow trails. Along these roads, the imaginative mind of the desperado devised many misleading tracks for the posse members to follow, causing them to lose more sleep and miss more meals than did Tracy himself.

The Courageous Women.

Though a few horseback, boat and buggy rides were stolen, Tracy traveled mostly on foot, demanding, with the air of a king, that men, women, and children do his will. He forced women to prepare his food, children to run errands, and men to serve as slaves at his command. Knowledge that Tracy, convict, robber, and murderer, was in the vicinity was sufficient to terrorize whole neighborhoods. Only those who followed closely on the news can appreciate the fright left on children or the terror of the Tracy scare on nervous people.

The effect, however, was not the same on all, for some women along the way not only exhibited fearlessess, they made practical suggestions to the pursuers and furnished valuable information on the geography of the country. An example illustrating the different natures of people occurred in the Lewis River area in Washington. A woman by whose cabin Tracy and Merrill had passed a few hours in advance of the posse served food to the pursuers. While ministering to them, surrounded by a number of her children, she anxiously inquired into the chances of the convicts visiting her home.

*"The children and I have not slept for two nights,"
she said. "My husband is at work and I don't know how
to shoot a gun, even if I had one."*

*When told that if Tracy and Merrill did show up, all
they probably would want was food, she did know what
she would do in that case.*

*"Let Mr. Tracy come and demand food, if he dares.
I'll poison him—that's what I'll do."*

*It was learned afterward that she procured a potent
poison and placed it in food which was saved for Tracy
and Merrill. But the fugitives never honored her with a
call.*

Tracy's Terrorizing Power.

*Tracy soon learned the value of his terrorizing
power, and made the most of it. Usually the first
announcement upon entering a residence was, "I'm
Tracy." The commands that followed were generally
obeyed to the letter, and the hypnosis of his threats often
lasted many hours after his departure. At the beginning
of the break, Tracy, then accompanied by Merrill, called
on J. Roberts in the city of Salem, and exchanged his
convict's uniform for a citizen's suit. It was not till the
middle of the next morning that Roberts worked up the
courage to go and tell the police. Pat McGuire, of Clark
County, Washington, was robbed by Tracy and Merrill
on Sunday morning, but officers nearby were not notified until in the evening.*

*Johnson, of Kent, who entertained Tracy all day and
rode a distance of some twenty miles to town to purchase him a revolver, did not throw off the spell and tell
the Sheriff until the next day. It was some time after his
liberation before Anderson was free from the influence
and able to talk intelligently of his travels with Tracy.
When Tracy was present and inquiry was made as to
his whereabouts, his involuntary hosts or captives
always made answer at variance with the truth, at
Tracy's suggestion.*

*There were those who dared to invite the conse-
quences of disobedience to his will, and in the list of*

those exhibiting such temerity belong the names of Charles Gerrells, the little daughter of Mrs. Akers, Mrs. Van Horn, and the Seattle delivery boy. Charles Gerrells, when given the two stolen watches, and ordered to take them into Seattle, convert them into money and buy revolvers, instead went direct to the Sheriff's office, delivered the watches and informed the Sheriff that Tracy was at his mother's house, awaiting his return.

When Tracy and Merrill appeared at the home of Mrs. Akers, near Monitor, Oregon, and ordered the family assembled while a meal was being prepared, one little girl broke away and informed the men working at a mill some distance away. While Tracy was partaking of a meal at the home of Mrs. Van Horn, she whispered it to a delivery boy, who promptly spread the news and had Sheriff Cudihee in front of the house before the outlaw had finished his repast.

It is to be remarked that servile obedience did not seem to elicit any particular gratitude or excite the admiration of Tracy. Anderson, who rowed his boat, carried his burden and performed all the functions of a menial servant, received no reward or encouragement at his master's hands, but was kept bound hand and foot when off duty. Young Gerrells, when first held up, was taken to the camp that had been left in charge of Anderson, bound with strings. The Gerrells boy's attention, upon arriving at camp, was attracted to Anderson by Tracy's remark, "Look at the pig."

Good Work by the Hounds.

The bloodhounds that followed Tracy's track—though they have been criticized for not running him down—were a source of annoyance to him. He told "Stoolpigeon" Ward, so Ward relates, that he would rather get a shot at a bloodhound than at a deputy sheriff.

When given a chance, the hounds did good work. Named "Track," "Bell," and "Don" by their handler, Guard E.M. Carson, they were skilled manhunters. A quarter of an hour after Tracy had left the Gerrells house, a hot trail was taken and the dogs were giving tongue freely, but they had gone only a few hundred yards when they came to a river and the baying ceased. Here Track had waded the river. Bell plunged in and swam half-way across, but as her mate would not follow, she turned back. Both dogs were hurried to a bridge below and crossed to the other side. The scent was taken up again, but the dogs had not proceeded far when they began sniffing and rolling in the grass. Carson's attention was called to the strange antics of his dogs.

"That's red pepper," he answered, "sprinkled by Tracy along his trail. It won't last long."

Soon they were again giving tongue in the direction of Lake Washington, and here Tracy, in order to reach the cover of the woods by the shorter route, had waded across the southern end of the lake, in places taking water up to his armpits. Bell, upon reaching the lake, again plunged into the water, this time followed by Don, and, by means of the scent left on the brake grown up in the shallow water, gave proof of how a dog can swim and follow a track.

Skirting the edge of Lake Washington is an electric car line, which connects Renton and Seattle. The track crosses the southern end of the lake on a trestle. Tracy, coming onto the road in the lake, climbed the trestle and walked ties. The dogs, upon reaching the trestle, were at their wits' end for a while, for it was too high for them to climb. They were helped up on the trestle by Carson and took the direction of Seattle. Their progress on the trestle, it soon developed, was slow, for they were unaccustomed to running on the ties, and their legs would go between the timbers. They were taken up by the first passing car and carried across the trestle, and, after following the trail half a mile farther, it was lost on the shore of the lake, where a dense forest extends down to the water's edge.

The dogs circled for a radius of a quarter of a mile, and, failing to find the track as darkness neared, they were called off for the day, leaving the hunted man wet, fatigued and without supper or provisions, to spend one of his most uncomfortable nights since the Gervais siege. It is probable that the dogs were thrown off the track on this occasion by his taking to the lake and following the edge of it a mile or more.

Though the bloodhounds, as well as the human man-hunters, failed to capture Tracy, they did their part in leash and out.

Sheriffs Handicapped.

The men to whom Tracy has been particularly annoying in his flight from justice have been the Sheriffs. It is they to whom people generally look to capture him, and the Sheriff of each county through which the outlaw has passed has regrets that Tracy came his way. Since Tracy has prolonged his stay beyond all expectations in King County, Washington, and put the county to an expense of more than $10,000, besides killing three and wounding another, Sheriff Cudihee has been the object of more or less censure, but it is only proportionate to the length of time Tracy has sojourned in his county, and the amount of mischief done. Through every county through which the outlaw passed there is to be observed a disposition to throw on the Sheriff more responsibility than belongs and to expect more than the bounds of reason will permit. Of course Tracy should have been captured, but it is difficult to say who should have done it. Sheriffs generally are not on an equality with Tracy in his particular line. A Sheriff's equipment usually consists of a revolver and a pair of handcuffs, and he is rarely ever practiced in the use of a rifle. Tracy carries a 1000-yard gun, and though not a "crack shot," does very good work with it. Another handicap to the Sheriffs are the posses they have to deal with. The large reward offered brings all kinds of people into the chase, and however reckless or incompetent the man, a Sheriff feels a delicacy in *sending him home. Sheriff Cudihee had fully his share of would-be Tracy catchers to deal with.*

Sheriff Durbin has been by some held responsible for not routing Tracy and Merrill out of the Gervais jungle the day they were surrounded. There were two companies of militia in the fields surrounding the woods, over which Durbin had no control. It is the duty of the Sheriff when he calls for troops in this state, to point out in a general way what he wants to accomplish and leave the matter of carrying out his wishes to the commanding officers. When the Sheriff pointed out to the officer Major Leabo the woods where Tracy and Merrill were concealed and told him the aid of his militia was asked to capture them dead or alive, the limit of his authority was reached, and it was up to Major Leabo to lead his troops into the woods or keep them on guard. The Sheriff was responsible only for his deputies.

In addition to all other kinds of problems, Sheriff Cudihee had the newspaper reporters to deal with. They were an intelligent lot of good fellows and kept the public thoroughly informed on what happened and didn't happen on the chase in King County, but they needed an official censor. More than once Cudihee's plans were prematurely published by over-zealous reporters, in the strife to be first. One of Cudihee's reporters met a deputy out of town and each looked suspiciously at the other. The reporter dodged behind a telegraph pole and the deputy jumped behind a bank. After an hour's peek-a-boo performance, the reporter opened fire, and kept it up until he concluded his antagonist was dead enough and left him for the hogs. The deputy afterward entered a complaint that the reporter shot in his direction.

WALTER LYON.

In addition to the Lyon article, the *Oregonian,* which was closing its book on the Tracy escape now that he appeared to be on his way to freedom, published several items dealing with the convict's lurid past. One was titled:

MURDERER FOR YEARS.
Tracy's Monstrous Record Before
He Came to Oregon.

The name Harry Tracy, under which the outlaw is extensively advertised, is an alias. His real name is Harry Severn. He was born in Missouri, and was 27 years old the 23rd of last October. Inquiries received for him at the Oregon Penitentiary reveal that he has operated in the Hole-in-the-Wall country, and over the Northwest generally. He is an escapee from the Utah Penitentiary, and is very much wanted in Colorado to answer for the murder of V.S. Hoy.

A letter recently received at the penitentiary from a Colorado officer, in response to a letter of inquiry concerning Tracy, gives a bit of his history. It says:

"Lant, Tracy and W.H. Brown, a mulatto, escaped from the guard at the Utah Penitentiary a year ago last October. They got away at the same time. Tracy held up the guard at the muzzle of a revolver, changing clothes with the guard at the same time. Tracy has no wife that I ever heard of, and none of his acquaintances have any knowledge of his being married, yet it would not be surprising if he had, as most of these outlaws have a wife somewhere in Utah. It seems as if Utah girls have a decided preference for outlaws as husbands.

Your last question: "Do you know any other of his pals?" I live near the state line of Colorado, Wyoming and Utah. It is a wild, sparsely settled section, and up to the time my brother was killed these outlaws were coming and going all times of the year. When V.S. Hoy was killed, there was a grand uprising all over the country by law-abiding people, and since that event we haven't seen or heard of the gang only in a general way. Without any by-laws, they are a brotherhood. They all know or know of each other, and when one of them as a stranger first comes to a neighborhood he knows who his friends are. When hotly pursued by officers, their

associations are broken up by their being scattered, cap-
tured or killed. Lant, Tracy, Johnson and Bennett were
pals at the time of the killing of V.S. Hoy. Bennett was
lynched, Johnson sent to the Wyoming Penitentiary for
20 years, you have Tracy, and the devil only knows
where Lant is.

J.S. HOY.

At that time, it should be pointed out, there were two outlaw
hideout regions called "Hole-in-the-Wall," one in Wyoming in
the Bighorn Mountain area, another in the high mesa and
desert country along the Utah-Colorado line. Butch Cassidy
and the Sundance Kid, who used the Wyoming hideout, had
recently fled to South America with their ill-gotten gains, while
the outlaw refuge referred to by the above letter was the one
along the Utah-Colorado line. In the note left for Sheriff
Cudihee, Tracy had said he was headed for Wyoming, but he
appears to have had no connection with the Butch Cassidy
gang.

A Vile Monster.

Another letter received by the jailer in Portland at
the time Tracy was arrested reflects something of how
he is regarded in Colorado, (the Oregonian *article con-*
tinued.) The letter is from the brother of the murdered
man:

"I saw in the newspaper dispatches that Tracy had
been captured and jailed, and again that he had made
another desperate attempt at escape. Tracy, Lant and
Johnson are the names of three arch villains who were
together when they killed my brother near this post
office, March 1, 1898. They were captured three or four
days later by citizens from Utah, Wyoming and
Colorado. To my call for help men came from all
around, and night and day kept up the chase until the
three were taken.

"There were so many men that the escape of the three
outlaws was impossible. The next morning after my
brother was killed, Jack Bennett, a pal of the three, was
taken and lynched, and that that act seemed somewhat

to satisfy the people's vengeance is the only reason I can give for their not hanging the murderous trio. Johnson was tried shortly afterward at Green River, Wyoming, for murder, and sent to the penitentiary for 20 years. Lant and Tracy were sent to the Roult County Jail to await their trial at the next term of the District Court, where they beat the Sheriff nearly to death, escaped, were recaptured, sent to Aspen for safe-keeping, where they did up the jailer and again escaped.

"There is no doubt but Tracy fired the shot from behind a rock, not more than eight or ten feet from where my brother stood, and killed him instantly. My brother at the time was looking the other way. The act was the most cowardly, foul assassination. Tracy is a case of total depravity. There is not a single redeeming trait in his make-up. He has forfeited all right to live. He is utterly reckless and thoroughly desperate, and has no regard for human life, conscience-seared, a vile monster, to kill whom ought to secure any man's eternal salvation.

"Don't trust him one moment. Chain him to an anvil; treat him as he treats others. Hanging is too good for him. I was the Justice of the Peace before whom their preliminary examination was held for killing Valentine S. Hoy, and it was my opinion, and the opinion of others present, that more heartless, indifferent, and hardened human devils never lived.

"Everyone now, while grinding his teeth, thinks that all three ought to have been taken out and hanged to the same beam from which Jack Bennett dangled. When you folks get through with Tracy, if he is above ground, we want him here. For that reason, and to put you on your guard, is why I write this letter.

J.S. HOY."

The final item published in the issue of the *Oregonian* meant to close out the subject, was titled:

Tracy's Mother.

It has been stated, apparently with the view of excusing Tracy's murderous break from the penitentiary, that he was flogged or he never would have made the attempt. The statement is entirely erroneous, as Tracy was never flogged in the Oregon State Prison. He and Merrill did both wear "Oregon boots," however, during the summer of 1899, when it was found out that they were in a conspiracy to escape in June of that year.

Tracy professes at times to have regard for his mother, but his regard is not of that kind that influences his actions in a way to please her. She wrote him regularly while he was in the Oregon prison, apparently trying to impart to him some cheer, but occasionally a lapse into an outburst of grief betrays her deep sorrow for the condition of a hopeless son.

In a letter received by Superintendent Lee for Tracy from his mother about the time of his escape, she says:

"My Dear Boy: My life is darkened with the sorrow that has come to us. Oh, why, why was it that my boy should ever do anything to be shut up in a prison! It almost set me crazy. They thought in time I would not feel so bad, but oh! the pain is there just the same as it was at first."

In a previous letter, she asked why her boy had changed his name, but Tracy never responded.

CHAPTER THIRTEEN
THE FINAL BATTLE

In a boastful mood after leaving the MacEldowney ranch, Tracy let the authorities know he was in the community, using a phone to call the sheriff and tease him about his inability to capture his man, ending the brief conversation with the consoling comment:

"You've done better than the other sheriffs, anyway. At least, you've talked to the man you want. Goodbye. I'm afraid you won't see me again."

Whether Tracy's statement that he intended to re-join the "Hole-in-the-Wall" gang in Wyoming implied that he was a member of the crowd of outlaws led by Butch Cassidy and the Sundance Kid, which recently had been in the news, was not established then or later. But in his present predicament, he was very much on his own.

Though he lacked confederates to support him now, he did not lack company long, for he picked up an eighteen-year-old boy named George E. Goldfinch near the railroad siding of Fellows, Washington, sixty-five miles west of Spokane. Later, the young man told how he was recruited.

Sunday afternoon, he'd been riding along on the prairie about ten miles south of Creston, Goldfinch said, when he was hailed by a stranger riding a big bay horse and leading a smaller sorrel. At first, he paid no attention, then the stranger kicked his horse into a run, cut the youngster off, and waved his rifle in an order to stop. Goldfinch did.

"I'm Tracy, the convict," the man said. "Who are you?"

"George Goldfinch," the young man gulped nervously. "Pleased to meet you—I think."

"I need food, rest, and water for my horses. Where's the nearest ranch?"

"Why, that would be the Eddy place, sir," the boy said, turning in his saddle to gesture at a set of buildings a mile or two away. "It's a bachelor spread, run by Lou and Gene Eddy, who are brothers."

"Perfect! I want you to ride ahead and tell them who am. I won't hurt them if they do as I say. Can you handle that?"

"Yes sir, I think so."

"Get moving, then."

Later, George Goldfinch told reporters that when he introduced Tracy to Lucius Eddy and his younger brother Eugene, who were taking their Sunday afternoon rest in the shade of the barn where they had been installing a hay-lifting device, ". . . there did not seem to be any unusual stir." But as his actions showed during the next few days, he likely was too excited himself to be a very good judge of the emotional state of others. Later, Lou Eddy would speak for himself:

> *When Tracy came to the ranch Sunday evening, he was accompanied by young Goldfinch. I was out working in the barn. The two went into the house and when they did not find anyone at home, they came out to the barn. The boy was in the lead. When they came, my brother and I were working. Tracy said:*
>
> *"You had better tell him who I am."*
>
> *The lad told us, and from then on we were at his service. He had his rifle with him. He said:*
>
> *"All three of you come along with me, for I have something for you to do."*
>
> *Of course, we went and let our work go. He first had me unsaddle his horse and feed the animal. The two boys had to go with him, and he always went behind. In nearly every case where he went he would say: "I guess*

I had better go behind." He asked me very closely as to the road to Sprague. The next thing, he wanted me to trade horses with him. He asked me what kind of horses I had, and I told him a 3-year-old colt and a 14-year-old mare. He said he did not want to trade if that was the case, and that he would wait at the ranch until his horses were rested. He said they had traveled a long distance and were tired, adding:

"I believe in taking good care of my horses, because I depend upon them for my escape."

He fed them regularly and was very good to them. He kept his horses in the little shed just east of the blacksmith shop and always had one saddled. That was so he could make a quick flight out of this section of the country, if it was necessary.

After we fed the horses that evening he wanted a revolver pouch, and in order to get one he went to my saddle and cut off one side. He said he would rather work at that in the house, so he took us all in with him. He said he would have us make it, but we did not know how.

He always carried his rifle or revolver. He said he had two revolvers, but we never saw but one. I believe he just carried one, and that is the one which was purchased at Tacoma by a farmer, whom he held up. In order to carry his revolver, he cut the front of his shirt open just at the top of the band of his trousers, and then put the gun through that hole. That kept it concealed. He then made a cartridge belt, saying he might have to use it a great deal while passing through this country.

After the work was completed, he cleaned up his rifle. He took the peep-sight from my brother's rifle and put it on his. After his gun was ready, he said he would go out and test the sights. He paced off 60 yards and shot at a knot in a pine board. The knot was not larger than a 5-cent piece, and he hit it as near the center as possible.

When he returned to the house, he handed me the gun and asked me if I ever saw such a smooth stock. Of

*course, all the loads were out of it, and Tracy knew I
could not do him any harm. He was always good-
natured, and did not seem to worry. When he was in the
house during the daytime, he would sit in the corner of
the kitchen near the window with his back to the wall.
He could see out of the house in nearly every direction
and could watch us. He would not sleep in the house at
night, and said he preferred the haystack. He made my
brother sleep with him, while I slept on the other side of
the house.*

*No, we were not uneasy while he was around, for we
knew if we did what he told us he would not harm us.
It interfered somewhat with our work. We woke up at
five o'clock Wednesday morning, and Tracy helped to
prepare breakfast. The longer he was with us, the more
he would trust us. The young lad was released Sunday
evening, but not until Tracy had instructed him that if
he told, he (Tracy) would kill my brother and I. He told
the boy that several times.*

*He took a bath and a shave while he was here, but
his rifle was standing against the wall near him while
he was at that job. He did not intend that we should
take him unawares. He did not take his shirt off this
time, but rolled it back when he wanted a bath.*

Again, Tracy's naive faith in young people was betrayed, for
the boy, George E. Goldfinch, disobeyed the outlaw's order not
to reveal his presence at the Eddy ranch by phoning the news
to Sheriff Gardner in Creston Monday afternoon. Compounding
the betrayal, young Goldfinch then acted as a guide, scout, and
strategic advisor to the lawmen, keeping them posted on what
was happening and carrying messages from group to group.

Although reinforcements had been sent for and would soon
arrive, five Creston residents—Constable C.C. Straub; Dr. E.C.
Lanter; Maurice Smith, an attorney; J.J. Morrison, a railroad
section foreman; and Frank Lillengren, a hardware store
owner—were determined to bring Tracy's violent career to an
end here and now.

Cautiously closing in on the ranch buildings where the outlaw had taken refuge for the past few days, the men saw Lou Eddy riding a horse-drawn hay mower in a sub-irrigated pasture near his house, signaled him to a halt, and engaged him in conversation. As Constable Straub talked to Eddy, he thought that the rancher looked very nervous. When a man whom the officer did not recognize emerged from the barn, Straub asked:

"Is that Tracy?"

"It surely is."

Following orders, Eddy drove to the barn, with the posse members carefully following behind. Tracy came out of the barn and began to help his host unhitch the team. He had left his rifle in the barn, but was carrying his revolvers. Suddenly he looked suspiciously at the posse members.

"Who are those men?" he demanded.

"Hold up your hands!" Constable Straub ordered before Eddy could answer. "We're officers of the law!"

Reacting instantly as always, Tracy jumped behind Eddy and the team, ordering the terrified rancher to lead the horses into the barn. When he did so, Tracy reached into the barn, seized his rifle, and snapped two quick shots at the constable and the posse members, who were holding their fire for fear of hitting Eddy. Though his shots missed, they made the posse members hit the dirt, giving Tracy time enough to dash headlong down the slope in a break for freedom.

With bullets whizzing all around him, he reached an outcropping of rocks, took refuge behind it, and began exchanging fire with the five possemen. As they spread out to get better angles, he realized that his situation soon would become untenable, so, crouching low, firing back over his shoulder as he ran, he bolted down the hill toward a field filled with ripe, waist-high wheat, which offered better shelter.

Suddenly he stumbled and fell on his face. He had been hit. Recovering himself enough to rise to his hands and knees, he managed to crawl the seventy-five remaining feet to the wheat field, moved into it, and disappeared from sight.

By now, it was growing dark. Soon reinforcements arrived in the form of twenty-five men under Sheriff Gardner from Lincoln County, a dozen under Sheriff Doust of Spokane

County, and Sheriff Cudihee from distant King County. Though all of them were brave men, nobody was so foolish as to follow Tracy into the wheat field and check on how badly he had been wounded.

The truth was, his wounds were serious. Hit twice, he had managed to crawl the seventy-five feet to the shelter of the wheat field. The first bullet had struck his right leg half way between the knee and the ankle, breaking both bones. The second bullet had taken effect in the rear of the same leg, midway between the hip and the knee, causing a flesh wound, the bullet lodging near the knee. Both wounds were bleeding freely. In a desperate effort to stay alive, Tracy stuffed his handkerchief into one wound, then cinched a leather strap tightly around his leg in an effort to prevent a fatal loss of blood from a severed artery.

Finding both attempts futile, he used the last of his remaining strength to place the muzzle of his biggest revolver to his head just below his right eye—and pulled the trigger.

The long, tragic drama was over.

Even though the surrounding law officers and possemen heard the revolver shot and guessed its meaning, they remained on watch outside the wheat field without attempting to enter it until after daylight the next morning. There, they found Harry Tracy lying on his back, stone dead from his own hand. A reporter who viewed the body wrote solemnly:

> *The body presented a horrible sight. It was covered with blood from head to foot, and the unsightly wound over the right eye was a ghastly one.*
>
> *As he lay in the wheat, his rifle, which had become famous, was by his side. His cartridge sack, which was made of buckskin, was found a short distance from him. It contained 150 rifle cartridges. Two boxes of revolver cartridges were also found near the sack, which he had carried since he was hunted near Seattle. His ammunition was not near him. It is thought that he was so weak that he believed he would expire before he could empty the chambers of his guns. Nine loads were found in his rifle.*

Taking charge of the body, Sheriff Gardner had it placed in a wagon owned by liveryman John McGinnis and rode with it to the town of Creston, eleven miles away. By the time the wagon reached town, word of Tracy's demise had spread like a prairie fire. Hundreds of people followed the wagon up the street to the mortuary, the *Spokesman-Review* reporter wrote, and from every corner shouts could be heard:

"Three cheers for Lincoln County!"

The town literally went wild. The mortuary doors had to be closed, and the crowd was asked to stand back. In what turned out to be a bad decision, Sheriff Gardner agreed to let a limited number of people in to see the body. That was when the trouble started. The reporter wrote:

> *Everybody wanted a relic, and most of them got it, for after a short time nothing was left but the body. Someone even picked up the clotted, blood-stained handkerchief, which had been used by Tracy to keep from bleeding to death. Before he could carry the awful relic away, he had to do it up in paper, as it was too wet to place in his pocket. Someone got the strap which had been pulled around his leg to keep him from bleeding to death. That, too, was soaked with blood, which ran from the upper wound.*
>
> *Many locks of hair were carried away, and in some places his head had been made bald. His trousers were cut into strips, and before they were divided they were cut into smaller pieces. Some of the men standing about the streets said that warrants should be sworn out for the arrest of people who were stealing the articles which belonged to the state. A good many warrants would have had to be sworn out. Many of Tracy's cartridges were divided among the members of the posse and to those who could get at the buckskin sack.*

The same issue of the newspaper detailing Tracy's death contained a story headlined:

DISPUTE OVER WHO TAKES BODY.
Cudihee Asks for the Remains, but Creston Holds Them.

DAVENPORT, Wash., Aug. 8—(Special.)—Tracy is still the chief topic of discussion upon the streets, and excited groups are contending over who is entitled to the reward. Some maintain that Goldfinch, the young man who notified the officers of the outlaw's presence at Eddy's ranch, is entitled to a large share, while others hold that the men who went in the field and brought the dead man out are entitled to it.

There is now a controversy over the possession of the body. Constable Charles Straub, of Creston, who was a member of the posse of five who first hailed the fugitive, has a telegram from Governor Geer of Oregon, advising him to hold the body until further orders. Cudihee presented a telegram from a King County Deputy Sheriff, stating that the Oregon executive had telegraphed instructing the Coroner and Sheriff to turn the corpse over to Cudihee. The Creston contingent will probably make a formal demand for the body.

Reward for Tracy's Capture.

State of Oregon	$1500
State of Washington	$2500
Brother of Guard Ferrell	$100
	———
	$4100

During the prolonged arguments over how the reward money should be split up, no one considered the fact that it had been Harry Tracy himself who had ended David Merrill's career, not to mention his own. So if any person deserved a reward for that much-desired service to mankind, it was he or his designated heirs.

As the critic reviewing the "Tracy and Merrill" drama following its opening at the Third Avenue Theatre in Seattle had predicted, young people wasted no time following the exciting example of the most glamorous outlaw of the era. Three days after Tracy's demise, a central California newspaper reported:

JUST LIKE TRACY.
Youthful Imitator of the Outlaw Is
Wounded and Kills Himself.

SAN JOSE, Cal., Aug. 9—A series of daring highway robberies, which resulted in the sensational death of one of the robbers and the wounding of a citizen, occurred on the Monterey road a little before 5 o'clock this evening. Two young men, apparently little more than boys in age, opened the proceedings by compelling an old lady who was driving along the highway near Edenvale to alight and deliver her horse and buggy to them. They then drove to E.F. Heples' store at Coyote, where they bought cartridges for a .32-caliber pistol. This they loaded, and immediately proceeded to hold up the proprietor and several bystanders, one of them holding the pistol while the other made the collections. From the till they got only $5 or $6, and from the bystanders about as much more.

From Heples' they continued toward Gilroy. Within a quarter of a mile, they met W.W. McKee, a sewing machine agent, accompanied by J.E. Roland. The highwaymen drew a shotgun and pistol and commanded McKee and Roland to hand over their money. McKee, believing he had met two boys on a lark, did not check his horses, and one of the highwaymen discharged his pistol. The bullet passed through a sewing machine cover and struck Roland in the fleshy part of the hip, inflicting a trifling wound. McKee lashed his horse into a run and was not further molested.

The robbers continued southerly to Stevens' store, a mile and a half from Heples', robbing two or three teamsters on the road of small amounts. They were just entering Stevens' store when they saw five or six armed men riding rapidly toward them. This was a posse consisting of E.V. Heples and the men who had been robbed with him. The robbers abandoned their jaded horses and started across a field toward the westerly foothills. A running fight ensued, in which one of the robbers was shot through the stomach. In emulation of Convict Tracy, he placed his pistol to his head, blew out his brains, and died almost instantly. The other threw up his hands and was taken into custody.

The robbers were George Tan and Fred Williams, each about 23 years old, who have been living in and adjacent to the town of Mayfield. Williams was wanted there on a battery charge, he having defaulted his bail. Tan is the one who killed himself after being shot.

The dispute over what was to be done with Tracy's remains did not last long. Though a deputy sheriff from King County claimed that he had received a telegram from Governor Geer of Oregon saying the body should be turned over to Sheriff Cudihee, who would accompany it to Seattle before sending it back to Oregon, some of Cudihee's critics said that this was an attempt on his part to repair the damage done to his reputation for always getting his man by failing to capture or kill Tracy during the outlaw's long sojourn in King County.

In view of the fact that three of his men had been killed, $10,000 in county funds had been spent, and that in several instances newspaper reporters and amateur bounty hunters had interfered with rather than helped the Tracy manhunt, Sheriff Cudihee, who had stuck to the chase to its very end, was justified in seeking some credit for being in on the kill.

In the end, a compromise was reached, with Washington Governor McBride saying that the coffin containing Tracy's body would be shipped through Seattle on its way back to Oregon, but could not be opened en route.

All that is wanted is positive identification of the body and proof that the reward is going to the right men. The payment of the $2500 offered will exhaust the *appropriation made by the last Legislature for such purposes.*

A duly certified coroner's jury reported that the corpse indeed was that of Harry Tracy, while a dispatch from Constable C.A. Straub named posse members Maurice Smith, Frank Lillengren, Joe Morrison, E.C. Lanter, and himself as the "right men."

Embalmed, placed in a plain wooden coffin, and put in a wagon heavily guarded by law officers and possemen, Tracy's body was transported from Davenport, the Lincoln County seat, southeast ten miles to Moscow, Washington, (later re-named Bluestem) where it was put aboard a Great Northern train bound for Seattle. Accompanying it not as an honor guard, but as possemen determined to get their share of the reward money, were Constable C.A. Straub, Dr. E.C. Lanter, and attorney Maurice Smith.

After two months of freedom, Harry Tracy was going home to the Oregon State Prison in Salem to serve out the rest of his sentence.

Lincoln County Historical Society
The posse that tracked down Harry Tracy.

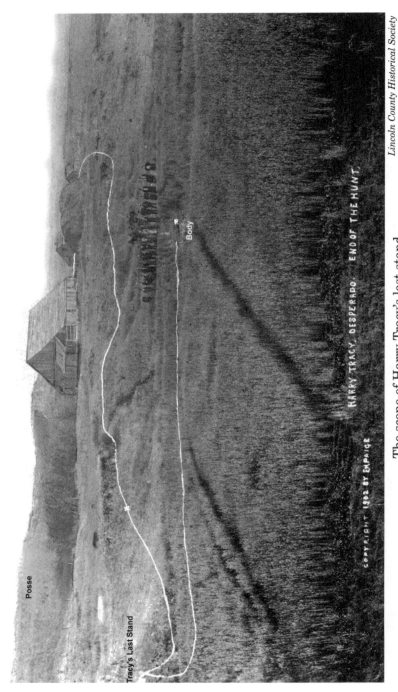

Posse

Tracy's Last Stand

Body

HARRY TRACY, DESPERADO. END OF THE HUNT.

COPYRIGHT 1902 BY EMPAIGE

Lincoln County Historical Society

The scene of Harry Tracy's last stand

Lincoln County Historical Society, Photo by E.H. Paige

The end of the trail for Harry Tracy.

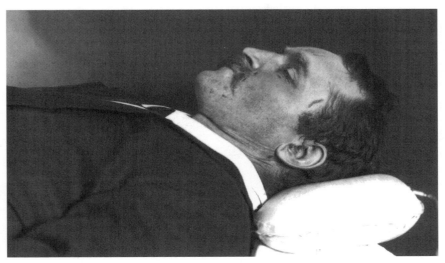

Lincoln County Historical Society

Wenatchee World

Harry Tracy stole these horses from the Lockwood Ranch, near Wenatchee, after spending the night with W.A. Sanders and Sam McEldowny at their ranch.

CHAPTER FOURTEEN
HOMECOMING

Seattle Aug. 9. (Special) Without a cartridge in the barrel or the magazine of Harry Tracy's famous 30-30 Winchester, the intimate friend on which he so often depended for the preservation of his safety, was used as a shield today to hold a large and excited crowd back from the convict outlaw's body. Handled by Constable C.A. Straub of Creston, the gun was pressed against a number of people at the Union depot to keep them away from the box containing Tracy's remains. Many of those who were near enough reached out their hands and touched the rifle reverently, as if they regarded it as an object almost equaling in point of importance Tracy himself.

Never during the bloody career of the convict since he made his escape from the Salem penitentiary was Tracyphobia witnessed in so virulent a form as when the Great Northern train bearing his lifeless body rolled into the Union depot yesterday at noon. Railroad avenue was jammed with a black mass of humanity from Marion street to Yesler way. All morning the sheriff's office was kept busy answering inquiries by the telephone as to whether the public would be permitted to get a view of the body. Under Sheriff Corcoran wired Sheriff Cudihee at Snohomish to learn whether or not the body would be exhibited, but received no answer.

When the train arrived, however, the crowd in waiting demonstrated the fact that plenty of people were willing to risk being disappointed.

As the train rolled into the station there was a rush forward, the crowd surging out on the track, directly in front of the engine, and strenuous exertions on the part of policemen, the depot master and a number of cool headed citizens were required to avoid accidents. Not waiting for the train to stop, a large number of people clambered upon the steps of the coaches and maintained their positions despite the efforts of the trainmen to remove them. It was afterward learned that a few had gone to Interbay and met the train, riding from there to the Union depot.

Attracts First Attention

Among the first to alight was Deputy Sheriff Nelson. A glimpse of his gun was sufficient to let the eager spectators know that in some way or other he was connected with the transportation of the remains, and he was asked more questions in a minute than he could possibly have answered in half an hour.

In a few minutes the familiar form of Sheriff Cudihee was seen to emerge from a car, and he at once became the center of attention. He was asked but one question:

"Is Tracy's body with you?"

In answer Cudihee simply nodded his head in the direction of the baggage car. There followed immediately a scramble for the baggage car.

Many remained by the side of the sheriff to inquire if there would be an opportunity of viewing the body. Cudihee answered that he feared the custodians would not consent to the box being opened. They were afraid of an attempt being made by an organized gang to steal the body and did not intend to take any chances of losing the reward. Henry Watson, of the undertaking firm of Bonney & Stewart, and Bert Butterworth, of Butterworth & Sons, held a private conversation with the sheriff to see if there was a possibility of the body being exhibited at their places of business, if only for a short time, but were informed that its custodians had steadfastly refused to permit the box containing the remains to be opened under any consideration.

Shortly after the train stopped at the depot, the body was removed from the car to the baggage room, pending its transfer to a Northern Pacific car for Portland. There was a hush as the box was borne to the baggage room by four strong men and then the crowd surged forward again. The look on their faces showed that they could hardly realize that the rude receptacle held the bullet-shattered remains of the man whose very name was sufficient to conjure up visions of terror throughout the whole of King county.

Accompanied by Claimants

Accompanying the body to Portland were C.A. Straub, constable of Creston; Dr. E.C. Lanter; Attorney Maurice Smith; and H.J. McIntyre, of Ravensdale. With the exception of McIntyre, who was along merely for the sake of the trip, these men will come in for a share of the reward. The 30-30 rifle was carried by Straub. The three men claiming a part of the reward kept close to the box in which the body was enclosed as it was carried to the baggage room and remained near it for more than two hours, until it was placed on a car for Portland.

As the crowd pressed too close, Straub pushed the people back with the rifle. One or two men shrank away as the death-dealing weapon touched them, but others laid their hands on it. Several remarked that they would like to be able to say they had touched the rifle carried by Tracy.

During the long wait for the train, members of the crowd engaged the custodians of the body in conversation. Detailed descriptions of the last encounter were what the auditors wanted, and every now and then a question was sandwiched in to draw out more clearly information regarding some small circumstance connected with the battle. Straub and Lanter were rather *reticent and showed an aversion to discussing the affair, but Smith was loquacious. He had just finished a bit of vivid descriptive work when a tall, red-headed man standing on the outskirts of the crowd shouted:*

"Say, young fellow, you talk too much. The whole gang of you did nothing entitling you to any particular credit. You shot from behind rocks, and there were five of you to one. There wasn't a one in the gang that had nerve enough to sneak into that wheat field on his stomach and see what the shot meant when Tracy committed suicide."

Puts End to Story

This sally was greeted by a titter, but no reply was forthcoming. However, the descriptive work lagged afterward and the crowd passed the time for a short while in examining and commenting on the box. It was a plain, oblong box of dark wood, lined with zinc. Where the zinc lining protruded and was flattened across the end, a band-like effect was produced.

When 3:45 o'clock came, the time for the Portland train to pull out, only about fifty persons remained at the depot. The men who are taking the body of Tracy to Salem seated themselves in one of the cars as soon as the remains of the convict were placed in the Northern Pacific baggage car. There is a rule prevalent on the railway lines that no guns shall be carried in passenger cars unless covered with some kind of wrapping. For this reason the 30-30 was placed under the seat. A number of people followed those who were in at the death into the car and insisted on seeing the gun. After making objection for a few minutes, Straub finally consented and produced the rifle.

"I want to say I have touched that gun; that will be some satisfaction," remarked Garfield Connell, the leader of a delegation from North Seattle, as he reached forth his hand and held it on the barrel of the weapon. Before Straub could replace the rifle in its former position, every person near it had laid a hand on it.

Lanter and Straub admitted that young George E. Goldfinch, who conveyed the news that Tracy was at Eddy's ranch, is entitled to a share of the reward. They say the boy had shown more courage than had a great many adults and deserved to be repaid for it.

"We are the ones who are to decide how the reward shall be apportioned," declared Straub. "We are all willing that that young Goldfinch shall come in for his share. Without his notification, none of the present party might have been within miles when Tracy met his death."

Asked in regard to the whereabouts of the two revolvers Tracy had, all the members of the party professed ignorance. Straub winked at Lanter and they vouchsafed the general information that they are somewhere in Lincoln county.

Details Fully Told

Asked to give an account of the battle in which Tracy received the wounds causing him to commit suicide, Straub replied:

"The Post-Intelligencer *has had full, fair and accurate accounts from start to finish since Tracy appeared east of the mountains. The description of what followed after we arrived at the Eddy ranch was particularly good. There is no detail of any importance that has not been touched on and nothing any of us could add would give any better idea of the last encounter than has already been contained in the* Post-Intelligencer. *We got the body aboard the train at Moscow last night at 10 o'clock and came straight through with it. We are going to Portland, from there to Salem."*

Shortly before the train pulled out, Joe Williams, brother of the deputy sheriff wounded by Tracy at Bothell, arrived at the depot and asked Straub to see the dead convict's rifle. It was handed to him and after a critical examination, Williams gave it back with the remark:

"That is the gun with which Tracy pretty near took my brother's life. I would like to have that gun as a curiosity."

Three small scratches on the stock of the weapon caught Williams' eye while he was examining it. After commenting as quoted, he drew attention to the scratches and said they were probably caused while Tracy was scrambling over a barbed wire fence.

Sheriff Cudihee is rather thin and much sunburned by his Eastern Washington trip. His eyes were bloodshot, showing loss of sleep and the mental strain to which he has been subjected.

"It's all over now, and I guess the rest of you are as glad of it as I am," he said shortly after the train arrived at the station depot. "That fellow Tracy was a wonder. He fooled me even at the last. I was fifteen miles away guarding another road when he committed suicide. The man could never have left that country alive. I do not believe he had the least idea of the dangerous position he occupied until the crash came.

"I don't want any of the reward. I simply made up my mind I would follow Tracy to the ends of the earth unless he was killed or captured in the mountains. The Goldfinch boy showed excellent judgment and a good deal of bravery and is certainly entitled to a share of the reward."

Are Prominent in Creston

The three men who are accompanying the body of the dead convict to Salem are prominent citizens of Creston. C.A. Straub, who was appointed to take charge of the remains by Gov. Geer, has a fine record as constable of his home town. Dr. E.C. Lanter is one of the leading physicians of Creston, while Maurice Smith has more than a local reputation as an attorney. All are comparitively young men and are known in their neighborhood as splendid marksmen.

In the accompanying picture, Constable Straub is seen holding Tracy's famous 30-30 Winchester. He is taking it direct to Gov. Geer, by that official's orders. At several places on the stock the bloody imprint of Tracy's fingers is still easily seen. Though rusty and worn-looking on the outside, the rifle is in splendid condition. The peep sight, which Tracy secured at the Eddy home, was returned to the farmer when the body of the convict was taken to Davenport.

When Straub, Lanter and Smith, with J.J. Morrison and Frank Lillengren, heard of Tracy's presence at the Eddy farm, they armed instantly. Without waiting for help, they hastened to the ranch and opened the fight. All are determined looking men.

Revolver Missing

A faint echo of the Tracy turmoil was heard in Sheriff Cudihee's office yesterday afternoon, when E.M. Johnson, of Kent, who was compelled to journey to Tacoma and buy the famous outlaw a revolver, appeared and asked for the return of the weapon.

He was much disappointed to learn that the gun is not in the possession of the local officers, but had been retained by Sheriff Gardner of Davenport. At Johnson's earnest solicitation, the under-sheriff wrote Gardner, calling his attention to the fact that the revolver belonged to Johnson, and asking for its return. The revolver was a 45 Colt's, and was among the weapons found near the desperado's body.

Still carefully guarded by three of the possemen who had been in on the kill, the remains of Harry Tracy headed south that afternoon, while the *Oregonian* used a final front-page box on the two-month anniversary of the story's first publication:

The body of Harry Tracy, the convict-murderer who eluded the peace officers of some of the most populous counties of Oregon and Washington, and was finally brought down by a shot from the gun of a country posseman, is now on the way to Salem. The body, with a cheap covering, is in a sealed coffin. There was no public exhibition along the route, and there will be none in the Oregon capital, if the petition of some of the state's most influential citizens can prevent it. It will probably be shown to the convicts, and it will be interred in the penitentiary burying grounds.

Although a local morning paper announced that, upon its arrival in Salem, there would be a public exhibition of the body at the morgue, such a storm of protest from friends and relatives of the slain guards broke over Governor Geer and other officials that the viewing was quickly cancelled, if indeed it was ever scheduled.

"For the beneficial effect that will result in the prison discipline," Superintendent Lee announced, "it will be arranged that many of the trusty convicts and probably some of the men within the prison will be permitted to view the body of their former associate."

Following this display, the remains were taken to the prison burying grounds, about half a mile distant from the main building.

LAST OF OUTLAW TRACY
REMAINS BURIED BESIDE THE
GRAVE OF MERRILL.

SALEM, Aug. 9—(Special.)—The body of Harry Tracy was received in Salem today from Davenport, Wash. The final chapter in the remarkable career of the multi-murderer was recited today when the remains of the criminal were buried beside those of his associate-in-crime, David Merrill, in the prison burying ground.

Tracy's body reached this city on the belated overland train at 11:20 o'clock this morning. It was accompanied to Salem by Constable C.A. Straub, Dr. E.C. Lanter and attorney Maurice Smith of Creston, Wash., from whom the body was received by Superintendent J.D. Lee, of the state penitentiary, after receiving the assurance that the casket contained the body of Harry Tracy.

No sooner had the rough box containing the remains reached the platform at the depot than a score of half-crazed relic hunters in a wild scramble separated themselves from the large throng that surged about the baggage car and with knives began the mutilation of the box containing the remains in order to get a mere splinter of wood that might serve as a souvenir. But for the prompt intervention of Superintendent Lee, who was on the ground, the box would surely have been hacked to pieces, and it was only by threatening the disturbers with arrest that the casket could be removed to the wagon without further molestation.

Attended by Farmer John Porter, of the prison, who was placed in charge of the remains, and the others, the body was driven direct to the penitentiary. Arrived there, the box was carried into the turnkey's room where, for the first time since the body left Davenport, the cover to the casket was removed. The body was positively identified as that of Tracy by Superintendent Lee, Warden Janes, Turnkey McCormick, and shop guards John Stapleton and Albert Steiner. The remains were viewed by about a score of persons outside of the prison officials and employees of the institution, in addition to a large number of the trusty prisoners, while many of those inside the walls were given the privilege of looking upon the remains.

While there were probably 500 people at the depot station drawn thither by curiosity, but a very few presented themselves at the prison to take a last look. When the body had been identified and the remains had been viewed by those who cared to, the casket was closed and removed to the prison cemetery where it was interred beside the body of Merrill. No service of any kind attended the burial.

Destroying the Body.

Before the interment, chemicals were introduced into the casket that will destroy the body. This will defeat the expected attempt to steal the body. In addition to this precaution, Superintendent Lee says the grave will be closely watched and a warm reception will await the visit of any mischievous visitors.

Tracy was not the bad-looking man that the circulars pictured him. While he had the prominent cheek bones, broad chin indicative of a rare determination, deep set eyes and protruding forehead, credited him in published pictures, still his features were not bad. Having been embalmed, the body was in a splendid state of preservation and it was not difficult to identify the remains.

The Washington men are desirous of retaining the famous rifle that was captured after the death of Tracy as a souvenir of their hunt, but at the urgent request of the Salem officials they surrendered the firearm, which it is proposed to have placed in the office of the Governor. The revolvers that were found on Tracy will go to the men who found the body.

CHAPTER FIFTEEN
UNANSWERED QUESTIONS

Following the burial of Harry Tracy beside his former friend, David Merrill, several disputes and questions remained unsettled and unanswered for some time. During their visit to Salem, three of the five posse members from Creston, who already had been granted $2,500 from Washington Governor McBride, filed a claim with the state of Oregon for the $1,500 reward it had offered for the capture of Harry Tracy, "dead or alive." Getting wind of their request, Sheriff J.H. Gardner, of Lincoln County, wired Oregon Governor Geer:

"Do not pay Tracy reward until other claims can be filed."

When informed of the telegram, Superintendent Lee, who had just given the three men a receipt for the body, told them that further negotiations would have to be deferred until it was decided who should be paid the money. He suggested that all the Washington claimants agree on a man to whom he could turn over the money until a decision was made on its final disposition, this relieving the state of Oregon any further involvement in the issue.

While agreeing to that expedient, pending a conference with their friends back in Creston, the three men did file a claim with Oregon Secretary of State Dunbar for $284.65, which represented the transportation costs for the trip to Salem and back home, as well as the embalming expense and the purchase of a plain casket, as directed by Oregon officials.

The question as to who had supplied Tracy and Merrill with the weapons used in their escape still was not answered. Merrill's rifle had just been found near Chehalis, Washington, by John Goff and Fred Runcorn, who had discovered it two hundred yards north of where the body was stumbled upon by Mrs. Mary Waggoner and her son, George, whose claim for a share of the reward money still was not settled. Lying in thick cover twenty feet from the road, it apparently had been thrown there by Tracy after he killed Merrill in their duel.

"It is a .30-caliber, model 1894, Winchester rifle," the news item noted. "There were no cartridges in the chamber or magazine and the gun was cocked when picked up. There are some rust spots on the barrel but otherwise the gun is in very good condition."

Regarding the rifle that was returned with Tracy's body by the Creston possemen, Superintendent Lee and Warden Janes of the state prison had serious doubts that it was the weapon with which Tracy had made his sensational escape.

"The rifle is a 30-30 Winchester of 1894 model, and is numbered 72,884," Superintendent Lee said. "The magazine carries nine cartridges, and one in the barrel. On top of the barrel and in front of the adjustable sights is the inscription '30-W.C.F.' This will aid in tracing the ownership of the gun."

Officials were inclined to believe that the rifle returned to them was the one Tracy took from the sheepherder near Ellensburg, and that the original gun was either destroyed, hidden, or perhaps thrown into the Columbia River, as Tracy had threatened to do.

"Warden Janes says there is no doubt that the Merrill rifle that has been recovered is the weapon that he had when the desperadoes escaped from the Penitentiary," Lee said. "At the time the body of Merrill was found near Chehalis, officers of the Oregon Penitentiary arranged to search for Merrill's rifle, which was believed to have been thrown away in the vicinity of the body, for it was not believed that Tracy would allow himself to be handicapped with an extra gun. Oregon officials will gain possession of the Merrill gun, and will endeavor to learn whence came the rifles that were delivered to Tracy and Merrill in the Penitentiary."

The fact that the rifle's magazine and chamber were empty when found, with the weapon being cocked, would seem to indicate that Tracy had ejected its cartridges, which he could use in his own rifle, though he would not wish to be burdened with an extra gun. But it does not answer the question as to who smuggled the weapons into the foundry.

In time to come, Harry Tracy, like all outlaws who have made a break for freedom and ruthlessly killed any person who stood in their way, became something of a legend in the Pacific Northwest. Other than the fact that he was known to have killed seven persons during his two-month flight—and probably murdered three or four more prior to going to prison—he really was not a bad person, many people said. He treated his horses well, was very polite to ladies, and had a naive trust in young people—which finally did him in.

As has been said of better men, we shall not see his like again. Which is probably just as well.

THE END

Afterword

This is not the book I set out to write. Originally, I planned to relate the lurid careers of a dozen or so Pacific Northwest outlaws I feel have been neglected by "colorless chroniclers" whose writings have not done justice to their dastardly deeds. My final chapter in the book was to be titled "Harry Tracy, Mad Dog Killer."

Based on articles by Stewart Holbrook, William McCleod Raine, and other regional historians, who had written about Tracy twenty-five to thirty years after the outlaw's death, the accounts were probably accurate enough; still, I did not feel comfortable with them, for I have long made it a rule to use primary sources whenever possible so that any errors I make will be truly my own, rather than copied from those made by other writers.

Fortunately, primary sources were still available in the form of microfilm reels of contemporary newspapers such as the Portland *Oregonian*, the *Olympian*, the Seattle *Post-Intelligencer*, the Spokane *Spokesman-Review*, the Walla Walla *Union*, and other regional newspapers.

After spending several weeks reading and making printouts of these accounts I sent my Caxton editor, Wayne Cornell, a sample of the material I had found, then suggested that we might have a book on Harry Tracy alone. After reading the material, he replied:

"The thing that makes Tracy especially interesting, I think, is the time frame in which the story takes place. The nineteenth century had just ended. The era of the outlaw gangs like the James boys and the Daltons was past. By 1902, most Americans believed the country had emerged from the rash and reckless frontier days.

"But just when everything started settling down in the West, along comes Harry Tracy—a new kind of badman—not a Jesse James—more like a prototype for Clyde Barrow. And Tracy cuts his path of death through Oregon and Washington—two Pacific Northwest states that had been among the peaceful areas of the West. Although he traveled mostly by foot and horseback, he profited from the improved road network and the increased population. He was never more than a few miles from a meal."

So we agreed that the Pacific Northwest Outlaws book I had just completed should be set aside while I did a book on Harry Tracy alone.

Early on, I discovered that two elements normally not considered in the writing of a non-fiction book must be taken into account here: the press and the public. Not only did the Tracy manhunt make sensational newspaper headlines daily for two months, but a number of glory-seeking reporters actually armed themselves and took part in the chase; some of them even exchanged shots with Tracy. As for the public, every literate person in the Pacific Northwest became as dependent on his daily fix of Tracy news as TV viewers a hundred years later would become addicted to tidbits from the O.J. Simpson trial. Both the press and the public became part of the story.

This being the case, I decided that a special technique would be required for writing the book: namely, the use of what the trade calls "dramatic narrative." Instead of telling the reader the outcome of an event, as most historians do, then going back and analyzing how and why it happened, I would take the reader back to the moment in time just before the event occurred, then let him move forward as he would do in real life to experience the event as it happened.

Though historical purists may call this a cheap fictional device used to sensationalize what is happening, the writer who applies it will say it is just as honest as the theorizing done by historians who analyze a person's motives without a shred of documentation.

For example, the much-respected regional historian, Stewart Holbrook, writing about Harry Tracy in an *Oregonian* article thirty years later, dismissed him as "a low-grade moron," pointing out that he held up streetcars instead of trains, bars instead of banks, and on one occasion when he robbed a store stole only postage stamps and small change. Yet it is a matter of record that whenever Harry Tracy took a family hostage and moved in with them for a day or two, his first request was for food, his second for the past week's newspaper—including the *Oregonian*—whose columns he would avidly peruse in order to learn what was being written about him.

If he indeed were a "low-grade moron," as Holbrook says, he was a literate moron. Or is that in itself an "oxymoron"?

Once I had decided that I would tell the Tracy story as the reporters and readers of the day wrote and read it, I knew that this must be strictly a "Chase Scene" book, beginning with the prison breakout, ending with Tracy's death and burial. Nothing at all had been written about Tracy before the prison escape; very little was written after his death. So the amount of Tracy literature available to readers who collect such material is very scant. Two dime novels, a couple of melodramas, two silent movies, and a handful of newspaper and magazine articles published over the years are all that exist—with one notable exception.

This is *Harry Tracy: The Last Desperado*, by Jim Dullenty, Kendall/Hunt Publishing Company, Dubuque, Iowa, 1989, 1996. Born and raised in western Montana, Dullenty majored in history at the University of Montana, began researching and writing about outlaws as far back as 1957, worked as a reporter for the Spokane *Daily Chronicle*, and wrote his first article about Harry Tracy in 1972. Later, he became editor of magazines such as *True West, Old West,* and *Frontier Times.* An authority on Butch Cassidy and the Wild bunch, in 1974 he helped start the National Association for Outlaw-Lawman History Association.

When I first met Jim Dullenty, he was editor of *True West* magazine and asked me to write an article on the Nez Perce

Indian son of Captain William Clark, whose existence I had documented in my book *Chief Joseph Country: Land of the Nez Perce*. Learning that he had published a book on Harry Tracy, I immediately bought and perused a copy, finding it to be the most complete and authentic book yet written on Tracy, his ancestors, his family, his companions, and his criminal record prior to June 9, 1902.

"Writing about outlaws is a challenge," Dullenty says. "Most outlaws did not write biographies and were not interviewed for news stories."

This was certainly true in Tracy's case, though from the lengthy conversations he carried on with the hostages he took—particularly the ladies—the assumption can be made that Harry Tracy would have been glad to tell his side of the story to a reporter if guaranteed safe conduct to and from the interview, plus a substantial remuneration for his time.

In his book, Dullenty speculates upon the causes for Tracy's crime spree, a matter I do not attempt to explore, for mine is a simple action story of a convicted criminal's flight toward freedom and the law's attempt to stop him. Dullenty is much more critical of Sheriff Edward Cudihee than I have been, but, as noted earlier, I also disagreed with Stewart Holbrook's statement that Tracy was "a low grade moron."

I do endorse Jim Dullenty's statement that: "Outlaw research has to be a labor of love. No great foundations or well-heeled associations pay for this work. Universities do not offer scholarships in outlaw research. States do not promote outlaw sites or activities as tourist attractions, although they should and perhaps some will start. Utah, for example, discovered how important the Butch Cassidy cabin site was after it was noted on Utah maps.

"Montana recently began noting the Kid Curry hideout site on its maps," Dullenty continues. "The Tracy Rock in north-central Washington state is a natural tourist attraction. It attracts tourists anyway, but the state should do more to make tourists aware of it. Outlaws were an important and integral part of western development."

Two things impressed me during the many weeks spent reading 1902 newspaper accounts of the manhunt. First, the quality of the writing done by the reporters following a long, exciting day during which they may actually have exchanged shots with the wanted man, is literate, grammatical, and vivid, assuming a degree of intelligence on the part of the reader that news writers today would not dare to do.

Second, the literacy of the public is remarkable; almost all people could and did read, receiving and absorbing a breadth and depth of knowledge not only locally but nationally and world-wide that I seriously doubt is equaled today, despite universal education and computer-networking. Even if the only teaching tools in 1902 were the McGuffey readers and most teachers the products of two post-high-school years of training at a "Normal School," people with no more than a fourth-grade education seemed able to read at the college level, while today we are struggling to achieve the reverse.

INDEX

THE AUTHOR

Bill Gulick

Bill Gulick is considered by many to be the dean of Northwest history writers. During a career spanning more than half a century, Bill has published five nonfiction books, nineteen novels, three dramas, five movie scripts and more than 200 articles and stories for newspapers, national magazines and television.

Manhunt: The Pursuit of Harry Tracy, is the fourth Gulick nonfiction book published by Caxton Press. The others, all still in print, include *Snake River Country*, *Chief Joseph Country*, and *A Traveler's History of Washington*.

Gulick's novel, *Roll On, Columbia,* an historical trilogy, was recently released by Colorado University Press.

A long-time Washington state resident, Gulick has won numerous regional and national awards. He was one of the founders of the Western Writers of America.

Bill Gulick books
From CAXTON PRESS

Snake River Country
ISBN 0-87004-215-7
15x12, 195 pages, cloth, boxed $39.95

Chief Joseph Country
ISBN 0-87004-275-0
12x9, 231 illustrations, 316 pages, cloth, boxed
$39.95

Traveler's History of Washington
ISBN 0-87004-371-4
9x6, 194 photographs, regional maps, 560 pages, paper
$19.95

Manhunt: The Pursuit of Harry Tracy
ISBN 0-87004-392-7
9x6, 256 pages, paper, $18.95

For a free catalog of Caxton books write to:

CAXTON PRESS
312 Main Street
Caldwell, ID 83605-3299

or

Visit our Internet Website:

www.caxtonprinters.com

Caxton Press is a division of The CAXTON PRINTERS, Ltd.

WC